Michael Sedgwick

Ward Lock Limited · London

Author	**Michael Sedgwick**	*For Christine*
Illustrator	**Mike Atkinson**	
Editor/ Designer	**Eric Inglefield**	
Consultant	**Michael Ware**	

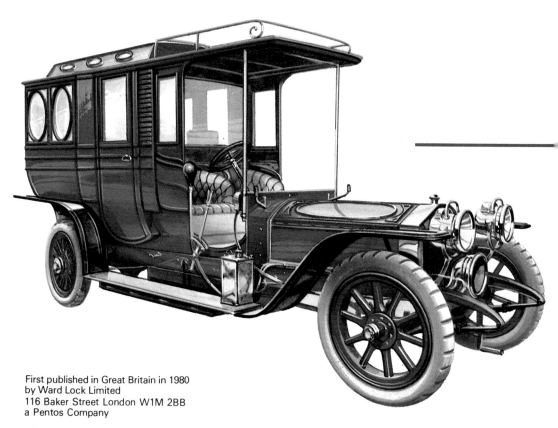

First published in Great Britain in 1980
by Ward Lock Limited
116 Baker Street London W1M 2BB
a Pentos Company

Designed and produced by
Grisewood and Dempsey Limited
141 – 143 Drury Lane London WC2
© Grisewood and Dempsey Limited 1980

Colour separations by Newsele Litho Ltd, Milan
Printed by South China Printing Co, Hong Kong

Sedgwick, Michael
  Veteran cars — (Classic car guides).
  1. Automobiles — History
  1. Title. II. Series

629.22′22′09041 TL15

ISBN 0-7063-6035-4

Contents

Introduction

In days when we are seeking a replacement for the internal-combustion-engined motor-car, it is sobering to reflect how rapidly it infiltrated our world. A hundred years ago it did not exist. Eighty-five years ago, Peugeot (then one of the world's top three) were happy to have turned out 72 vehicles in a twelvemonth. Yet within another decade, the Peugeot's native France had a potential of around 15,000 units a year, and the United States would break the 25,000 mark in 1906. When the world went to war in 1914, that country already registered over a million automobiles, and was adding half a million annually to the score. Britain had 132,000, with a yearly production potential close to 40,000. French industry was good for 50,000, and even Italy contributed some 10,000 a year. True, neither Japan nor Russia as yet manufactured seriously. In 1912, Greater London registered more cars than the entire Romanov Empire, but the importers of St Petersburg were bringing them in at the rate of 4,000 a year.

Admittedly, outside America the motor-car was still largely the preserve of the rich, and many countries were ill supplied with roads. The Ford succeeded in Asia, South America and Australasia partly because it was cheap,

partly because it was foolproof, partly because deliveries were undisturbed by the Great War–but chiefly because its suspension and high ground clearance were admirably suited to bush tracks. Without roads, the automobile could not make headway.

Consider France's leadership in the pioneering years. Latins were maybe less inventive than the Anglo-Saxon races. But they were also less hidebound in their attitudes (a 'horse lobby' never existed in France or Italy); they were also (in France, at any rate) beneficiaries of the admirable Napoleonic *routes nationales*. Germany was the nursery of the internal-combustion engine, and it would be fair to regard the Benz Velo as the first reliable automobile, but true German leadership would not be asserted until the advent of the Mercedes (pages 30–1) in 1901.

There were also Britain and America–the former the cradle of the Industrial Revolution and the world's iron-master, the latter the home of mass-production built up around the small arms and cheap watch industries. Yet neither led. The United Kingdom, indeed, inflicted a blanket speed limit of 20 mph (32 km/h) as late as 1930. Before that there had been the Locomotives on Highways Act of 1865, with its ossifying limits, not repealed until 1896. A railway-oriented economy, backed by turnpike trusts, were additional deterrents, which explain why early British road vehicles were commercial types–the coaches of Hancock and Gurney and the famed traction engines of Garrett and others. Thomas Rickett's steamers (page 14) were certainly private cars, but they were also technical dead-ends. A Bollée family could never have flourished in England.

Outside the big cities, the United States

◀ How we expect a Veteran to look. This 16hp, four-cylinder car is one of the bigger 1903 Panhards, with the layout made famous by this firm: engine in front, gearbox amidships, and drive to the rear wheels. Design is untidy: seven exposed banks of tubes form the radiator, driving chains are unprotected from road dirt, and there are no front doors, hood, or windscreen (the two latter were extras). Rear-seat passengers had a door, but it was in the tail panel, as on contemporary horsedrawn vehicles.

was roadless. It was left to the cycling clubs to proselytize the highways, a state of affairs which explains early cheap car design, and the immense publicity accorded to the early transcontinental marathons. Undoubtedly the industry could have turned out 10,000 mock-Panhards–or even mock-Mercedes–in 1903; there was simply nowhere for them to go.

In 1900 cars were still scarce: but most of the basic technical ideas existed. The automobile engine worked, and it delivered a creditable amount of power, if not very efficiently. Nor is it strictly true to assert that brute force was the governing factor. While racing units progressed from the 3 litres of the later 1890s to 17–20 by 1904–05, the little de Dion single of 1900 was running at 2,000 rpm and giving 6 hp from 500 cc, or 12 bhp per litre. Electric ignition and float-feed carburetters were established, and the mechanically operated inlet valve was soon to appear. Pneumatic tyres were general practice on lighter cars, and some designers, notably the Lanchester brothers, had broken loose from the old concept of the horseless carriage. For all the influence of the *système Panhard*– engine in front, gearbox amidships, and drive to the rear wheels–people were still making cars with rear engines or front-wheel drive. Such geniuses were no anticipators of Porsche or Issigonis: design was strictly functional. Engines went at the back because this was the simplest way to motorize a dog-cart or buggy. Front-wheel drive was another rudimentary form of hippomobile-to-motor conversion, as found on the Lohner electric (page 27) or the strange Pullcar (page 47) as late as 1907.

Further, right up to 1905, if not later, the question of motive power was unsettled. Steam and electricity bulked large. They were, after all, known (and harnessed) monsters long before Gottlieb Daimler and Karl Benz translated the ideas of Beau de Rochas and Lenoir into the motor-car engine as we know it today.

There were other attractions, such as greater dependability. There is nothing to go wrong on an electric, while the slow cold-starting rituals of steamers–even in 1909 it could take 35 minutes on a Stanley (page 59)– were at least sure, and preferable to the ignition and mixture headaches associated with internal combustion.

Then there was the matter of silence. An electric makes no noise; nor, its burner whistle apart, does a steamer, while by direct-coupling the latter's engine to the axle, and mounting the generator at the rear, one could also eliminate smell. The internal-combustion engine vibrated furiously: the price of the little de Dion's efficiency is a tumult which telephones its way up the steering-column. Above all, there were no gears to shift.

In this era of synchromesh and two-pedal automatic, it is hard to comprehend the hurdle of double-declutching, especially on constant-speed engines with no 'gun' to administer during a shift. Much ingenuity–often mis-placed–would be directed towards the elimin-ation of this headache. There were simple planetary transmissions which circumvented the dreaded 'side-grubbing of the teeth', there was belt drive such as that retained by Delahaye (page 29) well into the 20th century, and there were primitive multi-cylindered creatures such as the 1902 CGV, supposed to dispense with a gearbox alto-gether. No wonder that steam and electricity hung on as long as they did, especially after Serpollet mastered the paraffin burner and did away with the bulk and weight of solid fuels.

Electricity's demise was inevitable, on grounds of range. Batteries were almost as bulky as coal, so the system was soon confined to town runabouts. The advent of electric starting on 1912's Cadillacs was the final nail in the coffin.

Steam sat it out longer, though (Serpollet apart) most of the significant makes were American. Here too, range was a problem, for in pre-condensing days water consumption was formidable. Light runabouts such as the Locomobile (page 26) carried only enough for 20 miles (32 km), though later condensing systems improved substantially on this. Fur-ther, the steamer's excellent acceleration and hill-climbing powers were offset by the limit-ations of the boiler. A Stanley's 50 mph (80 km/h) could not be sustained for any length of time without a halt to build up pressure. Nor did one ever like sitting on a boiler working at 200 psi or more. Finally, steamers needed more skill to get the best out of them. And as with the electric, self-starters were the last straw.

As for mainstream development of the internal-combustion engine, it is fair to say that the first 15 years of our period (1885–1900) were devoted to making the machine work, the next ten to making it work reliably, and the 1910–14 period to the attainment of perfection. Though there was, of course, a great gulf fixed between the Rolls-Royce, which started 'on the switch' and wafted one up to a remarkably silent 60 mph (100 km/h) and the model-T Ford with its idiosyncratic cold-starting habits, jerky progress, and re-luctance to surmount really steep hills in

The structure of very early cars was like that of the horse carriage; the 1897 Cannstatt-Daimler's engine lived in a box like a 'meat-safe' attached to the rear.

A lightweight tubular chassis and wire wheels characterize the 1903 Humberette; front engines were general practice by then.

either of its two forward gears. For less than £200 in Europe, or, say, $900 in America, one did not expect refinement, even if by 1916 trans-Atlantic buyers were dispensing with crank handles and acetylene generators.

The motor-car was taking shape. The most important advances of the early period were the *système Panhard*, the pneumatic tyre, electric ignition, and the mechanically-actuated inlet valve, key to adequate engine control over a wider rev-band. Other developments – the high-speed engine, monobloc casting (which meant shorter and stronger crank-shafts), and the selective gear shift – were logical developments. So was shaft drive, which eliminated both the slip- and stretch-prone belt and the chain, the latter's tedious maintenance schedule involving boilings in Russian tallow! Ackermann-type steering was already established: the perilous centre-pivoting front axle was found only on the earliest horseless carriages, notably the 1897 Cannstatt-Daimler (pages 20–1).

In the age of the Mini, it has become fashionable to decry the Panhard arrangement as a space-waster. So it is, especially when allied to a hefty inline six like the 1910 Napier (pages 62–3). But the governing reason for its adoption was weight distribution. The Benz was inherently tail-heavy, and while this was irrelevant at the speeds of which the vehicle was capable, higher velocities, allied to short

wheelbases, poor roads, high centres of gravity, and solid tyres, rendered the Panhard configuration imperative if the motor-car were to succeed. It would also wean the vehicle away from its horse-carriage origins, though to the end of our period (in Europe, at any rate) chassis and body were still regarded as separate entities.

Pneumatic tyres were both vital to motoring, and its persistent early bugbear. On the one hand, they smoothed out the ride, permitting higher speeds. On the other, they were the automobile's prime limitation as dependable transport over long distances. The divorce from hippomobile practices meant front and rear wheels of equal diameter, and thus the end of duplicate spares, but throughout our period a tyre life of 2,000 miles (3,200 km) was considered good. The quick-detachable wheel, a 1907 innovation, was not generally used in Europe until 1912–13, and gained little head-way in America, where the rising incidence of female motorists would ensure the retention of the more manageable fixed wood type with demountable rim as late as 1931.

Electric ignition heralded the variable-speed engine. The original hot-tube species had been simpler than magnetos (always a closed book to the layman) and independent of batteries, the Achilles' Heel of early coil systems. It did, however, involve a tedious starting ritual. Also high winds (and bad

By 1913 cars were more manageable. A lady driver might, however, find the 12 hp Rover hard to crank from cold.

bumps on the road) could blow it out.

So in 1905 one still motored hopefully. The motor-car was tricky to start, and not over-controllable, with its limited rev-band: the usual maximum was about 1,200 rpm. Gear changing was difficult, while cone clutches had to be propped out with a block of wood overnight. Of amenities there were few: weather protection consisted of a cape cart hood and a windscreen. There were no instruments on the dash, and lighting came from an acetylene generator on the running-board. The light was excellent, but the system very vulnerable to rough roads.

Problems of maintenance bulked large. They did more to restrict the spread of auto-mobilism than the actual cost of a vehicle—or its attendant tyre bill. 'Motor servants' were almost a necessity.

The real trouble was that the motor car ingested as much dirt as it showered over passers-by. The elaborate undershielding effected by Spyker (page 65) was a palliative, but on the early American steam and gas buggies, and on early European *voiturettes* like

the Decauville (page 22) the 'motion' was wholly exposed. It was also under-lubricated, drip-feed systems being messy, and calling for constant attention. Under-oiling spelt seizures: too liberal a manipulation of those fancy brass oilers on the dash laid a smokescreen. Even in 1910, valve gear was often exposed, while gaskets and oil seals were not very effective. The combination of poor lubrication, and the abrasive effects of dust meant de-carbonization at 1,000-mile intervals, a labor-ious affair with fixed-head engines. Not the least of the advantages claimed for the Knight sleeve-valve motor was that it would cover large mileages between decokes.

Cleaning was a chore. Paint and varnish had to be wiped down after every journey, and renewed at yearly intervals. Brass called for constant polishing and there were chains to clean and boil. Nothing was standardized—so much so that among the recommendations put forward for a 'gentleman's motor house' was a screw-cutting lathe. (Cadillac's 1908 standard-ization test, when three cars were stripped and their parts scrambled before reassembly, created a furore in Europe.) As for garages, these were scarce, and all too often staffed by graduate blacksmiths and cycle dealers who used the local motorist's Benz or Wolseley as a training-ground. Good public transport, however, sometimes helped: British Hotchkiss owners were offered a 24-hour parts service from the Paris factory in 1910.

By 1914, many of the early problems had been solved. Pressure–or at any rate, semi-pressure–lubrication had banished the sight-feed oiler, wheels were detachable, and moving parts better protected from dust, itself on the wane thanks to wider use of tarmac. High-speed engines were gaining ground, and even the average touring unit would run up to 1,600–1,800 rpm. The majority of cars could be had with electric lighting, and Cadillac's electric starter would have become general practice by 1916, but for the war. As it was, in America only Ford held out against it to the end of our period. There was better flexibility, too.

Here the remedy was more cylinders, and thus less shifting. The prentice sixes of Napier and others were bedevilled by the absence of crankshaft balancers, a Lanchester contribution of 1909. One made a six by adding a couple of extra cylinders to a four, and the price of an easy walking pace in top was a tooth-shaking vibration further up the speed range. Crankshaft breakages were common, too–so the six went into temporary eclipse until a new generation of inexpensive Americans, (Buick, Hudson, Studebaker) made their appearance in 1913–14. The vee-eight, with its combination of compactness and flexibility, had been launched on the 1910 de Dion, and Packard followed up in 1915 with a successful V12.

What vital problems remained unsolved? In Europe, a cheap car had yet to emerge. Not so in America, where Ford's single model policy and moving assembly line had rendered outputs of half a million identical cars a year viable. The Europeans had two solutions, neither of them wholly successful.

Today a £175 ($875) Morris sounds a bargain, and it still seems reasonable value by the standards of 1939. But £175 was a lot of money in 1913, and what one got for it was a small four-cylinder engine, maybe electric lighting, and a cruising speed of 30–35 mph (50–60 km/h). The wheels would be detachable, but one still had to crank–and there were only two seats. To make it a four-seater would be asking too much of 15–18 bhp. We were a long way away from the Family Ten of the 1930s.

The other solution was the cyclecar, a barbarous contraption for graduate motor-cyclists. Just about the only uncivilized device omitted on it from the early nineties was tube ignition. To a noisy motor-cycle engine would be added cable-and-bobbin steering, belt drive (not always with a free-engine clutch) and plywood construction. One's reward was a £100 automobile capable of an unreliable and comfortless 50 mph (80 km/h).

Brakes, likewise, lagged behind. A 1914 Prince Henry Vauxhall with its lights, starter, wider rev band and excellent handling would in other respects be acceptable today. It can hold 70 mph (112 km/h), the multi-plate clutch is sweet in action, and what enthusiastic driver cares a fig for synchromesh? But its brakes–alas and alack! For a car weighing about $1\frac{1}{2}$ tons in road trim, there are a footbrake working on a drum behind the gearbox, and a handbrake working in drums on the rear wheels. The former, if liberally used, is a fire hazard, and can do dire things to the driveline. The latter will give you some interesting turns in the wet. Four-wheel brakes had already been tried by more than one maker, but since only Argyll (pages 72–3) used a proper coupled system, the improvement was minimal. Oreste Fraschini of Isotta Fraschini, indeed, admitted that his objective had been faster cornering on the circuit!

Also unborn was the cheap closed car. As long as composite body construction obtained –and Edward G. Budd's all-steel sedan did not see the light of day until 1916–a closed body cost more, weighed more, and killed performance. It is well to remember, too, that the 35 bhp of today's emission-stifled baby sedans was the norm for a 3-litre in 1914. Thus closed coachwork was reserved for formal carriages and 'doctor's coupés'.

Variety, however, was infinite. An Englishman in 1914 could take his pick, from £90–100 cyclecars up to big brutes like the 100 mph Isotta Fraschini (page 78). If he fancied steam, Stanleys were available, and Arrol-Johnston had acquired a manufacturing licence for the American Detroit Electric, now with a mock-Renault bonnet full of batteries. The Le Zèbre (page 60) had only one cylinder: but for £900-odd ($4,500) you could have an eight-cylinder de Dion, all 7.8 litres of it. And even on the real monsters, annual tax was £25 ($125) a year, insurance was not compulsory, and there was no driving test. One just had to remember that–in modern parlance–the footbrake was the hand-brake, and 'revs' did not extend much beyond what we would now term a fast idle.

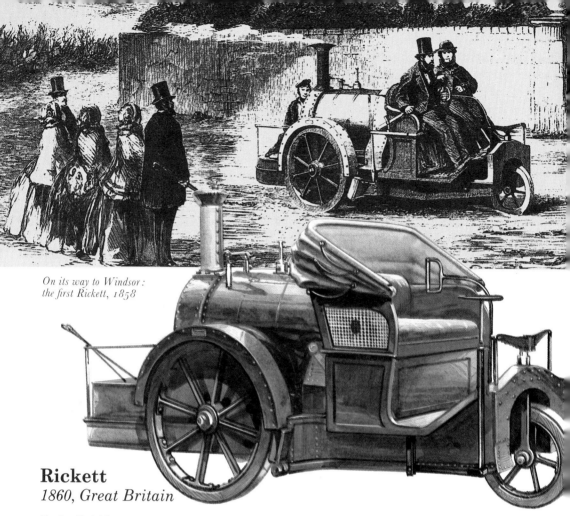

On its way to Windsor: the first Rickett, 1858

Rickett
1860, Great Britain

Early British road steamers tended to be coaches for public transport rather than private cars. An interesting exception, however, was the machine illustrated above. It was constructed at the Castle Foundry, Buckingham, by Thomas Rickett, one of three or four such vehicles for which he was responsible. His first, made in 1858 for the Marquis of Stafford, is recorded as only a moderate success, though the Prince of Wales showed interest. The car was also demonstrated at Windsor in the presence of Queen Victoria, having arrived from Buckingham under its own power.

Rickett's cars were three-wheelers, with drive to the rear wheels, initially by pitch chain, though a direct-coupled transmission was found on this example, commissioned by the Earl of Caithness in 1860. The driver and two passengers sat on a bench at the front, from which the vehicle was steered, braked, and reversed, the stoker occupying a platform at the rear. Mechanically, the Rickett was a road locomotive, even down to the horizontal boiler. Economy was hardly a strong point: a 90-gallon (450-litre) water supply sufficed for a mere ten miles (16 km), and coal consumption was estimated at 6–10 pounds (2.7–4.5 kg) per mile. Further, the weight in road trim was no less than 2½ tons. In spite of this, the machine comfortably exceeded its design speed of 10 mph (16 km/h), touching 18 mph (29 km/h) on occasion. The steel-spoke wheels seen in the illustration were later replaced by wooden ones, less destructive to road surfaces.

Lord Caithness was clearly of an engineering bent, and in any case the vehicle was destined for his estates in the North of Scotland, too thinly populated to attract any vocal opposition. In August, 1860, he successfully drove his car from Inverness to Thurso, a distance of 150 miles (240 km), accompanied by his wife and the Rev. William Ross. Rickett himself served as stoker. The Earl continued to motor happily in his remote fastnesses until the passing of the Locomotives on Highways Act in 1865 restricted such activities.

Benz
1885, Germany

If we owe the modern internal-combustion engine to Gottlieb Daimler and Karl Benz, the latter must rate as the automobile's true father. Daimler's interests were wider-ranging, and embraced railway and marine engines and stationary machinery.

The son of a locomotive driver from Karlsruhe, who died of pneumonia contracted while on duty, Benz had a hard struggle, training first as a locksmith and then as a locomotive engineer before setting up on his own in 1871. Though he had a two-stroke engine running by 1880, his finances were always insecure, and it was not until two years later that backing from Max Rose and F. W. Esslinger enabled him to pursue his experiments without constant anxiety.

The 1885 three-wheeler reflects some advanced thinking. Though he would later adopt the automatic inlet valve, Benz favoured mechanical actuation for the prototype: he also discarded wind-prone tube ignition in favour of a trembler coil from the start. The horizontal single-cylinder engine was mounted in a tubular frame, with the head pointing forward, and the crankshaft exposed at the rear. The flywheel was also set horizontally. Primary transmission was by belt; a side lever slid this onto a fast pulley when pushed forward, and onto the loose one when pulled back. Brakes were limited to a simple block-type working on the countershaft, and the invalid-carriage-type front fork was unsprung.

Despite a very low output – the first trials gave $\frac{3}{4}$bhp at 400 rpm – the Benz ventured onto the public roads in 1886, attaining 8 mph (12 km/h). It was, however, useless on hills, and by 1888, when deliveries began, such refinements as a two-speed gear and front springing had been added. Four-wheelers were in production by 1893, and by the end of the 19th century the breed offered reliable if slow transportation. A total of 572 new Benz cars found buyers in 1899, and the 600 mark was passed a year later.

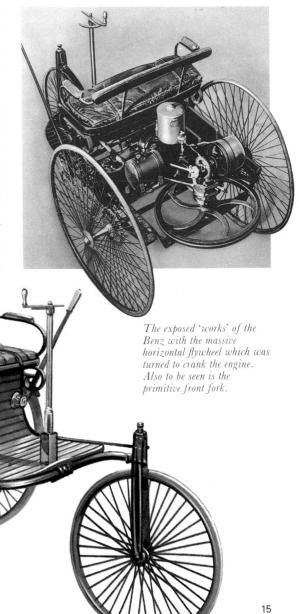

The exposed 'works' of the Benz with the massive horizontal flywheel which was turned to crank the engine. Also to be seen is the primitive front fork.

Amédée Bollée

1885, France

Although the work of Benz and Daimler was as yet unknown outside Germany, across the border in France the Bollée family, bell-founders of Le Mans, had been developing a series of steam road vehicles since 1873. These varied enormously, from small 'brakes' for personal transport up to the formidable *Marie-Anne* of 1879, a six-wheeled road locomotive rated at 100 hp and capable of hauling 80 tons on the level.

Amédée Bollée senior's first effort, *L'Obéissante* (1873), was good for 25 mph (40 km/h), and featured not only a two-speed sliding-type gear, but two-man operation, the driver being assisted only by a stoker at the rear. In 1876 he built a vehicle with all-independent suspension, a front vertical engine, and a differential back axle. Shaft drive came in 1880, by which

time Bollée had appointed a German agent and had orders for 23 vehicles on his books. Unfortunately, the press spread rumours that he was selling to the German Army (bitterness still ran high only a decade after French defeat in the Franco-Prussian War) and French interest faded away. Amédée, however, persisted with some lightweight steam brakes said to do 42 mph (60 km/h).

His son and namesake, at the age of 18, had taken a hand in the game, designing the neat little runabout illustrated below for his personal use – surely the world's first sports car. Its double-acting two-cylinder, slide-valve engine was front-mounted, with a longitudinal crankshaft, and shaft drive to the rear wheels. The car weighed only 1,410 lb (640 kg) and attained 25 mph (40 km/h). He built a second example for his grandfather, which made the Bollées the world's first four-car family, since both Amédée senior and his second son Léon had their own. The two young Bollée brothers would turn to the internal-combustion engine during the ensuing decade.

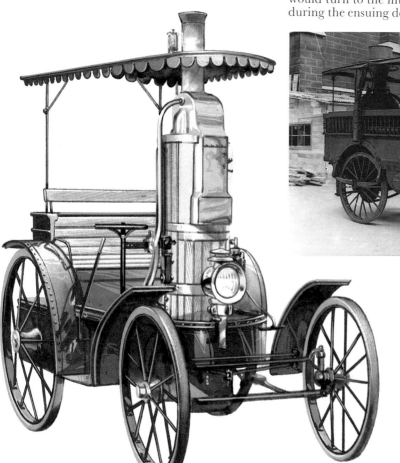

As a contrast with his son Amédée's 'sports car', the elder Amédée Bollée's 'L'Obéissante' of 1873 is more in the commercial vehicle idiom favoured by earlier British experimenters; it is what would now be termed a brake for eight or nine passengers, rather than a car for the owner-driver. The vehicle is now displayed in the Conservatoire des Arts et Métiers in Paris.

Duryea progress: the brothers' entry for the London-Brighton Emancipation Run, 1896. Unlike the 1893 prototype, this is not a converted horse-buggy, though the engineering is little changed.

Duryea
1893, United States

In later life the Duryea brothers, Frank and Charles, quarrelled bitterly over their respective contributions to the automobile. In any case, their 1893 prototype now preserved in Washington's Smithsonian Institution was not America's first gasoline-powered vehicle: that honour belongs to the 1891 Lambert. The Duryeas, however, founded the industry by setting up a company to manufacture automobiles in September, 1895.

The basic idea stemmed from Charles, who in 1890 was marketing bicycles made for him by a Massachusetts firm. With $1,000 (£200) financial backing from a certain Erwin Markham, he purchased a secondhand horse-drawn phaeton, which he proposed to motorize on Benz lines, with a horizontal engine and flywheel: Duryea feared that a vertical layout would adversely affect the steering. Burner ignition and a variable friction drive were planned.

Unfortunately, neither engine nor car would work, so during 1892 Frank Duryea was hired. Under his guidance this true horseless carriage was made to function. Charles's two-stroke concept was replaced by a four-stroke single, with automatic inlet valve and low-tension battery ignition. Transmission was by a system of three separate friction clutches giving two forward speeds and a reverse. Shifts were controlled by up and down move-

ment of the steering tiller, but the rear axle was unsprung, the carriage's original transverse full-elliptic spring being retained at the front.

The brothers' second car, built in 1895, was used for experiments with pneumatic tyres, ahead of the European pioneers. On solids, it also won America's first automobile race, from Chicago to Evanston, Illinois. In 1896 the Duryea company succeeded in turning out 13 identical cars for sale, now with belt drive on Benz lines. The basic Duryea theme was continued for several years in three- and four-wheeler forms, latterly with horizontal three-cylinder engines. One of these early Duryeas (complete with armoured fuel tank) became the first motor machine-gun carrier in 1901, while between 1902 and 1906 the make was built under licence for the British market in Coventry.

Neither Duryea brother was associated with any of the big American makers. Frank left to join the Stevens Arms and Tool Company in 1901, producing the limited-production Stevens-Duryea car. Charles's ventures included the odd Buggyaut high-wheeler of 1908, with two-stroke engine, friction drive, and true central control, enabling it to be driven from either seat. As late as 1916 he was still trying to promote obsolete high-wheeler designs in delivery van form.

17

Panhard
1894, France

To Émile Levassor we owe the layout of the internal-combustion automobile as it was understood for over half a century – an engine at the front, transmitting its power via an amidships-mounted gearbox to the rear axle. (The Bollées, of course, had already applied such principles to steam cars.) The *système Panhard* would be the model for the motor-car for the remainder of the 19th century, while the 'miraculous Mercédès' which supplanted it from 1901 onward was merely a more sophisticated development of the original theme.

The origin of the Panhard concern was a woodworking firm, Périn et Pauwels, established in 1845. Forty years later, the founding partners were dead, and René Panhard, who had replaced Pauwels, brought his friend Levassor into the company. Among Levassor's friends was Édouard Sarazin, who had lately acquired the French rights to the Daimler patents. When he died in November, 1887, these passed to his widow, whom in due course Émile Levassor married.

Levassor began his automobile experiments in 1889; he displayed no interest in belt drive, but tried amidships and rear locations for the engine before finalizing the layout in 1891. At this stage (and up to 1895) exposed gears still featured, cooling was on a total-loss basis, and unlike Benz, Levassor preferred burner ignition. Though solid rubber tyres had replaced iron in 1892, steering was by tiller, the wheel appearing on racers in 1895, and on production models two years later. Final drive was by side chains, while wheelbases were short and the centre of gravity high – a combination that would encompass Émile Levassor's own end.

With the birth of racing in 1894, the tempo quickened. Paris-Rouen was more a reliability trial than anything else, but the best Panhard performance on this occasion, an average speed of 11.1 mph (17.8 km/h) compares interestingly with the 15 mph (24 km/h) achieved by Levassor over the 732-mile (1,170 km) course of Paris-Bordeaux-Paris in 1895. By 1896 the original vee-twin engines of Daimler type had given way to vertical two- and four-cylinder units, the latter rated at 8 hp. By the turn of the century, Panhards of a nominal 12 hp were capable of nearly 50 mph (80 km/h).

Levassor, however, would not live to see the full triumph of his creation. In September, 1896, he set off on his last race, the 1,068-mile (1,700 km) Paris-Marseilles-Paris. His car collided with a dog and overturned, causing injuries to which he succumbed the following year. The company outlived him by 71 years, though there is a certain irony in the reflection that these pioneers of the 'conventional' automobile were among the first to dedicate themselves whole-heartedly to front-wheel drive, which they did in 1946. It is even sadder to record that the vicissitudes of their intriguing little Dyna first drove them into the arms of Citroën, and then, in 1967, into oblivion.

A youthful C. S. Rolls with his 1898 racing Panhard. Noteworthy are wheel steering and pneumatic tyres.

The controls of a 1903 7 hp Panhard, showing the make's characteristic 'barrel' controls on the steering wheel.

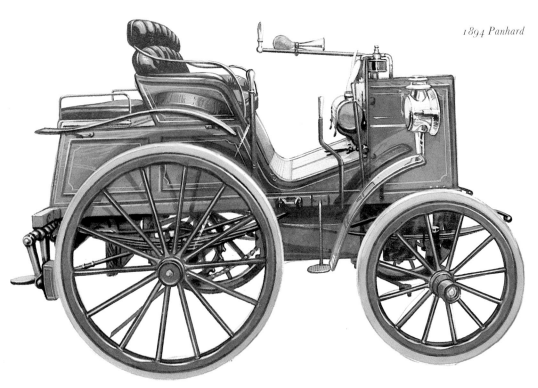

A World War I photograph of the Abbé Gavois with his Panhard, by then nearly a quarter of a century old, and which he himself had bought secondhand in 1894!

Léon Bollée Tricar
1896, France

1896 Léon Bollée Tricar

Some of the hazards of the early motor-car were highlighted by Émile Levassor's accident in 1896 (see page 18). Something lower and lighter was clearly desirable. The 1896 Léon Bollée tricar had at least both these merits: weight was a mere 448 lb (200 kg). In the 1897 Paris-Dieppe race Jamin's example averaged 25.2 mph (40.3 km/h), as against the 24.6 mph (39.4 km/h) of the big de Dion steamer, and the 23.1 mph (36.9 km/h) of the fastest Panhard.

Refinement was, however, totally absent. Here was a tandem-seater with single driven rear wheel, based on a steel-tube frame. The passenger sat in front, vulnerable to any accident. Of springs there were none: the single-cylinder horizontal engine with its burner ignition was rear-mounted. The driver's right hand controlled a small steering-wheel: his left coped with a spade handle. This, when pushed forward, slid the driving wheel back to tighten the belt: rearward movement loosened it, while rotation of the handle selected the three forward speeds. The footbrake worked directly on the flywheel, and only the barrel of the cylinder was finned, hence overheating was common. No clutch was provided: one 'paddled off', in motorcycle style.

A rousing and noisy 30 mph (50 km/h), however, presented no other problems, and the Bollée carried all before it until racing rules were amended to raise the minimum weight limit for *voiturettes*, and to stipulate side-by-side seating for the crew.

Cannstatt-Daimler 4 hp
1897, Germany

Though Gottlieb Daimler had motorized a boneshaker bicycle and had a primitive four-wheeler on the road in 1886, he was slower off the mark than Benz with series production. It was not until 1895 that Daimlers began to appear in any quantity; this early type was made until 1901.

Despite its wheel steering, the Daimler was primitive in every other way, resembling a horsedrawn carriage minus shafts and horse. Unlike Benz's cars, it used tube ignition, while the steering was of non-Ackermann type with centre-pivoting front axle, even if this were no hazard at such low operating speeds. Brakes were likewise somewhat equestrian: a pedal-operated wooden block on the countershaft supplemented by a spoon device on the rear wheels. The engine, an inline twin, lived in a box like a meat-safe at the rear. Four pulleys attached to the crankshaft transmitted motion by four flat leather belts to the countershaft, and thence to pinions meshing with toothed rings on the rear wheels. Cooling water was fed to the inside of the hollow flywheel. The coil springs at the rear were interposed between chassis and body: the engine, in an angle-iron frame attached to the latter, suffered from up-and-down movement on rough roads, accentuating the tendency of the burners to blow out.

1897 De Dietrich 9 hp

De Dietrich 9 hp
1897, France

Even though the combination of front engine and rear-wheel drive was gaining acceptance by 1897, not everyone was content with the *système Panhard* (see page 18). The de Dietrich, designed by Amédée Bollée junior of steam-voiturette fame for the famous Franco-German railway equipment makers, was afflicted with alarming complexities.

The twin-cylinder automatic inlet valve engine was mounted horizontally with the heads pointing forward, but the transmission of its modest output pursued a devious rearward course. A belt on the nearside of the countershaft had the usual fast and loose pulleys, on which four gears meshed with four further gears on a parallel shaft incorporating a differential. By this time the driveline was aft of the wheels, so any remaining power which had survived the transmission journey now had to come forward again via bevel gears and short universal-jointed shafts to a second pair of bevels! Even then the drive had to be turned through 90 degrees to a final set of bevels incorporated in the wheels.

The de Dietrich also had tube ignition, total-loss cooling from a water tank under the front seat, and a sight-feed lubrication system which coped with only one of the engine's main bearings. The pedal-operated reverse had to be held in by continuous pressure. Later improvements included proper tubular radiators (1898), chain final drive in 1901, and electric ignition by 1902. A total of 500 had been sold by the end of 1901. The car also did well in commercial form: a 3½-ton truck built in 1899 attained 9 mph (14 km/h) and could climb a 1-in-9 gradient with full load.

◀ *The rear doors give access to the Cannstatt-Daimler's twin-cylinder engine.*

1897 Cannstatt-Daimler 4 hp

21

Decauville Voiturelle
1898, France

De Dion Bouton's own light car did not make its appearance until 1899, but their high-speed engines were already being used in motor-tricycles and light cars. One of these was the Decauville *Voiturelle*, with its independent front suspension, which operated by a system of sliding pillars coupled by a transverse spring; the rear end was totally unsprung. Decauville devised a twin-cylinder engine by mounting a pair of aircooled de Dion cylinders fore and aft on a common crankcase, set below and behind the seat. The transmission consisted of two pairs of exposed (and unlubricated) pinions meshing with the crown wheel, the entire assembly, according to a contemporary critic, 'rattling like a mowing machine'.

The tubular frame rode on cycle-type wire wheels, and steering was by tiller, but the gear lever was mounted centrally on the floor and a hand wheel on the driver's right engaged with a shaft running down to the crankshaft, enabling the vehicle to be started from the seat.

The result was a side-by-side two-seater weighing only 595 lb (270 kg), and on the 1899 *Tour de France* the Decauville averaged 21.1 mph (33.7 km/h) over 1,350 miles (2,160 km) to win its class. Nor were ordinary customers dissatisfied. One testimonial published in a catalogue runs succinctly, if ungrammatically: 'Smoked cigarette, turned handle, and took me home like a tiger'! Decauvilles were made under licence in Germany under the Wartburg name.

Pennington Raft-Victoria
1898, United States

In these early years, the motor industry provided a ready opening for imaginative, hard-selling eccentrics, notably the American Edward Joel Pennington. For over 20 years he promoted improbable ideas on both sides of the Atlantic. There were a motor-cycle alleged to have done a 58-second mile in 1895, 'long-mingling spark' ignition, 'unpuncturable' pneumatic tyres, and engines capable of running on 'ordinary lamp oil', some of which induced Britain's wouldbe monopolist Harry J. Lawson to part with £100,000 (then half a million dollars) for the rights. Pennington's tricar with its ultra-long-stroke (62.5 × 305 mm) twin-cylinder engine and primitive fuel injection had been one of the sensations of 1896.

Two years later the inventor was back with an equally bizarre four-wheeler. The combination of front-wheel drive and rear-wheel steering was odd enough, even if by now the engine (either a single or a twin) possessed orthodox coil ignition. Transmission consisted of a primary chain, with final drive by rope (later a twisted belt was used) to the front axle. Steering was by a vertical push-pull tube on the driver's right, and only the body was

One half of the Decauville's independent front suspension.

1898 Decauville Voiturelle

sprung. The fuel injection was a notorious frier of plugs, frustrating Hubert Egerton's attempt to drive the car from Manchester to London. His supply of 48 spares had given out by Nuneaton! For all its much-vaunted low build and a tempting 95-guinea ($498) price, the 408 firm orders announced by Christmas, 1898, soon faded away.

An early effort by E. J. Pennington in England: the fearsome 1896 Tricar, with primitive fuel injection and his own patent 'puncture-proof' tyres. Even more passengers than those shown in this photograph were allegedly carried on some occasions, though the car's endurance on the road was dubious.

1898 Pennington Raft-Victoria

Saurer
1898, Switzerland

Anti-motoring elements persisted in Switzerland for many years. Thus it is not surprising that series production of Adolph Saurer's heavy-oil machines was undertaken under licence by Koch in Paris.

One critic dismissed the design as 'little more than putting an industrial motor into a carriage', and the formula was the typical horseless carriage style: unequal-diameter wheels, solid tyres, and tiller steering, replaced by a wheel on the second prototype, illustrated here. The big single-cylinder, horizontal opposed-piston engine, which lived at the rear, turned at 500–600 rpm, and tube ignition was used. Power was transmitted to the rear wheels via a three-speed gear and central chain, though on production Kochs this later gave way to spur gears.

The Saurer was designed to run on crude oil, and was 'highly recommended in districts where it is difficult to obtain petrol'. The price of such colonial virtues was excessive noise and exhaust smoke, and a slow cold-starting technique which involved liberal priming.

This 'did not matter in the case of a car driven by a servant or workman', but appealed less to owner-drivers. Kochs, however, found buyers in the British, Dutch and French colonies, one being Madagascar's first car: a fleet of six was in use there in 1900. Though Saurer marketed private cars until 1914, their main interest was (and still is) heavy trucks.

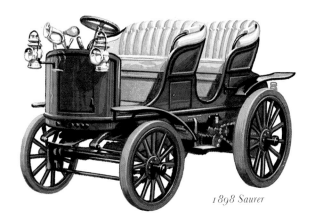

1898 Saurer

De Dion-Bouton 4½ hp
1900, France

By the turn of the present century the modern
light car was emerging. By the end of 1902 de
Dion-Bouton had made 33,000 of their single-
cylinder high-speed engine, were selling 2,000
voiturettes a year, supplying motors to countless
motor-cycle and car firms, and had a formidable backlog of orders.

When Benz and Daimler had been content
with 500–600 rpm, de Dion units ran at over
three times this speed. They were also vastly
more efficient–nearly 2 bhp from 250 cc in
1896, while the first car units extracted 3.5 bhp
from 402 cc. True, a rear engine might seem a
retrograde step in the *système Panhard*'s heyday;
so did the *vis-à-vis* seating of pre-1902 de Dions,
on which front passengers faced the driver and
obstructed his view. But the vehicle was
simple; it was also foolproof.

The basis of the car was a tubular frame, at
the rear of which the single-cylinder engine
was set vertically: on early models only the
head was water-cooled. Drive was transmitted
to the rear wheels via a two-speed constant-
mesh gear with separate expanding clutches.
The weight was carried on a tubular dead
axle, curved to pass below the final drive

*Before the days of the honeycomb radiator,
badges were rarely seen on cars. de Dion-
Bouton mounted their emblem on the side, and
the brass script at the front.*

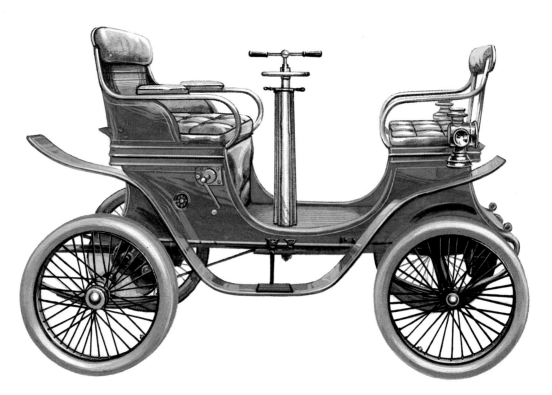

The bonnet on this modernized de Dion is a dummy: the game is given away by the side-mounted starting handle.

housing bolted to the frame. Ignition was by a coil of non-trembler type.

Driving was simplicity itself. The absence of a conventional clutch eliminated that all-too-familiar 'side-grubbing of the teeth', and lubrication was taken care of by a hand pump, given a quick squirt to four positions at 15–20 mile (20–30 km) intervals. In place of a hand or foot throttle, de Dion used a decelerator which actuated a transmission brake when depressed to its limit. On such a compact machine a reverse was scarcely necessary, but a pedal-operated device was added early in the car's production life.

Even the first $3\frac{1}{2}$ hp cars could exceed 20 mph (32 km/h), and the enlarged $4\frac{1}{2}$ hp of 1900 was appreciably faster. In 1900 the makers claimed that their clientele included five princes, two dukes, nine marquises, and nineteen counts and countesses. Light vans were available: one

firm of brewers even operated a 'product-mobile', on which the sidelamps were shaped like beer mugs and the driver sat inside a mock bottle, the label taking the form of a sheet of transparent glass – surely the world's first curved screen! The engine was listed in marine form, selling for £100 ($500) complete with mounting frame and reverse gear. A branch was opened in New York, offering complete cars for as little as $800.

Inevitably conventional influences moved in. Dummy bonnets had been seen on the rear-engined cars by 1902, while later that year the power unit was moved to the front, and subsequent singles could be had with orthodox, sliding-type three-speed gearboxes. The basic two-speeders, however, retained their following (notably in the medical profession) and were still being made, automatic inlet valves and all, as late as 1910.

Locomobile Steam Runabout
1900, United States

If the internal-combustion engine was already accepted in Europe for light cars, America was not so firmly committed. Here the role of such vehicles was limited to town work, and the same buggy-like structure with its piano box body on a light reach-bar frame sufficed, whatever the motive power. Some firms even offered a choice of gasoline, steam, or electricity.

Designed by the Stanley brothers, who had then sold their patent rights for $250,000 (£50,000), the Locomobile was a very early example of true volume production, sales building from 750 in 1900 to a peak of 2,750 two years later. W. M. Letts's London agency managed to unload 400 in two seasons. This was not surprising, since for £190 ($950), later cut to £150 ($750), the little runabout offered silence and a 20 mph (32 km/h) cruising gait, with no gears to shift. The 'works' con-

sisted of a vertical fire-tube boiler below the seat, and a two-cylinder simple engine driving direct to the rear axle by chain. The driver's right hand coped with engine and burner controls, steering was by tiller, and a pedal-operated band brake worked on the rear axle. In a disaster situation one reversed the engine, though if the chain broke, all means of slowing down ceased abruptly.

Snags were numerous. The burner was lit by a firing iron which had to be heated over a stove. If the fire went out on a journey, bundles of petrol-soaked rags were a poor substitute. The 15-gallon (75-litre) water tank gave a range of only 20 miles (32 km) between refills, and Hubert Egerton reckoned that on his British end-to-end drive of 1900 he had consumed the equivalent of five tons of the liquid. The entire motion was exposed, and road dust was never the best of lubricants. No wonder Locomobile elected to switch to the internal-combustion engine in 1903, though a year earlier they and their principal steam rivals (Mobile, Toledo, and White) had accounted for more than half the cars registered in New York State.

Lohner-Porsche
1900, Austria

Electrically-powered vehicles provided a choice of gears, and remained popular for much longer with the urban motorist, though the majority of such vehicles were chauffeur-driven broughams. Jacob Lohner, an old-established Viennese coachbuilder and supplier of coaches to the House of Habsburg, took the logical step in 1896, when he launched into self-propelled machinery to the design of a youthful Ferdinand Porsche.

Initially the concept was quite simply that of the *avant-train*, on which the steering axle of an existing horse-drawn carriage was replaced by an electric motor with spur gear drive to the front wheels. The batteries were housed under the coachman's box, four

An example of early four-wheel drive, this Lohner-Porsche fire engine was operating in London in about 1910. Similar ones were in use in Vienna.

forward speeds were provided, and an operational range of 25–50 miles (40–80km) was claimed.

In 1900, however, Porsche improved on this by mounting the motors in the front hubs, thus eliminating a complex drive train. For greater traction, four-wheel drive was offered, this doubling output from five to ten horsepower. A special tandem-seated car with streamlined nose was used by the designer himself to take the Semmering Hill Climb record, though this 10-kilometre uphill run at maximum speed represented the limit of battery endurance. Such was the load carried that this sprint car turned the scales at around three tons. On electric cars, power brakes served the same function as a steam car's reverse. There was also a special generator switch to enable the batteries to be partially recharged while coasting downhill.

From 1902, Porsche turned his attention to 'mixed' systems on which a petrol engine drove a dynamo to power his hub motors. This coped with charging problems at the price of further complexity, and though his Mercédès-Mixte cars ran in sprints, the future for both this type and for the Lohner-Porsche electric lay in the realm of commercial vehicles. Among types announced in 1908 were a rear-drive electric ambulance of conventional 'bonneted' appearance for Hanover, and a series of front-wheel drive fire engines for Berlin.

Serpollet Double Phaeton
1900, France

Léon Serpollet's steam cars featured a flash-type boiler in which water was pumped into a red-hot serpentine coil and converted instantly into superheated steam. The small quantity of water in the boiler at any given time made for greater safety: in addition, heat was generated only when power was required.

Serpollet had built a primitive tricycle in 1887. Two years later, he and Armand Peugeot attempted to drive an improved version from Paris to Lyons. The 290-mile (465-km) journey took a fortnight and involved more than one complete rebuild! By

1891 Serpollet had progressed to an Acker-mann-steered four-wheeler, and in 1896 he evolved a successful paraffin burner to permit the use of liquid fuel. Financial backing from the American Frank Gardner led to series production in 1898, and among 1900's clients was the Shah of Persia.

In 1891 Léon Serpollet was accompanied by Ernest Archdeacon on a pioneering drive from Paris to Lyons with his three-wheeler.

Left, below: the formidable brake which was driven by Ernest Archdeacon in the 1894 Paris-Rouen Trial, the ancestor of motor-racing.

Serpollets were more practical than Loco-mobiles. Both water and fuel were pumped automatically to the generator in properly metered proportions, and the car would run 100 miles (160 km) between refills. By placing his engine underfloor amidships and thus not integral with the driving axle, Serpollet avoided problems of unsprung weight, though driving chain and differential were, as always, exposed. A Serpollet could be fired up from cold in ten minutes. Later cars had auxiliary donkey pumps to maintain pressure when stationary in traffic. Performance was well up to internal-combustion engine standards, with an easy cruising speed of 25–30 mph (40–50 km/h).

Arrol-Johnston 12hp
1901, Great Britain

Even in the 19th century, local transportation requirements were being met. Scotland's appalling roads bred the dog-carts of George Johnston, T. Blackwood Murray and Norman Fulton, which were conceived in 1895 and in full production by the turn of the century. By this time Murray and Fulton had left Arrol-Johnston to found the rival house of Albion.

1901 Arrol-Johnston 12 hp

The Arrol-Johnston current up to 1905 was a true horseless carriage, with solid tyres and unequal-size wheels, usually delivered in varnished wood finish. The entire power pack was mounted horizontally underfloor; it consisted of a two-cylinder, water-cooled engine with opposed piston. The connecting-rod of one worked directly on the crankshaft, the other through a rocking lever. Ignition was by low-tension magneto, and both primary and final drives were by chain. Early Arrols were tiller-steered, but by 1901 a wheel had been standardized: this tilted to give easier access to the driving-seat, while on the bigger six- and eight-seaters, the car was conducted from the second row of seats. Arrol-Johnstons were started from the seat via a long rope with a handle attached. The possible consequences of a backfire are interesting to contemplate.

The maker's slogan was 'No noise, no dirt, no smell, and no vibration'. According to Johnston, he had devised a special blend of rubber which gave his tyres as good a ride as pneumatics. The cars cruised at a leisurely 12–15mph (19–25km/h). They were old-fashioned even then, but the high ground clearance had its advantages, and one owner claimed to have averaged 10,000 trouble-free miles a year (16,000km) over a six-year period.

Delahaye Type-0
1901, France

In France, Charles Weiffenbach—who was Delahaye's chief engineer for 47 of the company's 52 years—pursued the same objectives as George Johnston with his Arrol-Johnston in Scotland. The cars were not dissimilar in external appearance, with their varnished-wood dog-cart bodies, solid tyres, and underfloor-mounted horizontal engines, though Weiffenbach preferred a steel-tube frame, and his transmission arrangements followed Benz lines, with primary belts and side-chain final drive. Ignition was by coil.

By this time belt drive was old-fashioned, though it had its followers. One Delahaye enthusiast observed that 'a child can change the speeds noiselessly', pointing out that new belts cost ten shillings (50p) and could be fitted by any owner. The rest of the specification was orthodox enough, with pump cooling, a front-mounted tubular radiator, and three forward speeds. By 1900 wheel steering had replaced the handlebars of early cars. Buyers had the choice of 2.5-litre and 3-litre twins or the 1.3-litre single (illustrated below), weighing 800 pounds (400kg) in chassis form and credited with 20mph (32km/h).

Sales were respectable. By 1898, Delahaye had delivered 600 cars, and 250 of these Type-Os found buyers in three seasons. Already, the company was showing a serious interest in commercial vehicles, always a major part of their subsequent activity. The latest 1902 Delahayes had front-mounted engines and side-chain drive in the Panhard manner, but the traditional belt-drive types figured in truck catalogues as late as 1904.

1901 Delahaye Type-O

Mercedes 35 hp
1901, Germany

Wilhelm Maybach's Mercedes was the automobile sensation of 1901. If one draws modern parallels, it was the Rolls-Royce and Ferrari of its day, making a spectacular appearance in the 1901 Nice-Salon-Nice race with a winning average of 36.63 mph (58.6 km/h) over a long and hilly course. It rendered the Panhard – if not the Panhard system (see page 18) –

obsolete overnight, and within two years such firms as Star in Britain, Berliet in France, Martini in Switzerland, and Fiat in Italy were turning out convincing imitations of the design.

New departures were, of course, pressed-steel frames, honeycomb radiators in place of the Panhard's clumsy, unframed, nest of tubes, mechanically operated inlet valves, low-tension magneto ignition in place of burners, and a selective, gate-type gearchange instead of the progressive quadrant. None of

The 'office' of an early Mercedes. As a hand throttle was fitted, there are only two pedals, but the selective 'gate' gear change is visible, as is the sight-feed lubricator on the dash. Oil sidelamps of horse-carriage type sufficed.

The three-pointed star that is still the emblem of today's Mercedes-Benz.

Mercédès Jellinek, who gave her name to the Mercedes motor-car.

◄*Old and new design: an early 35 hp Mercedes (right) with a contemporary twin-cylinder Panhard (left). The contrast in radiators is noteworthy.*

these was entirely new. Daimler of Germany had fitted honeycombs on their 1896 truck and on their little-known PD *voiturette* of 1899. In this latter year, the 24 hp Phönix-Daimler racer featured a pressed-steel chassis and gate change, though its short wheelbase and high build gave it a well-substantiated reputation for vicious handling. And even if a Mercedes engine turned at little over half the speed already achieved by de Dion's tiny singles, it offered a high degree of engine control with its combination of valve gear, ignition, and Maybach's efficient float-feed carburetter. The lower centre of gravity made it safer to drive than the old Panhards.

Its dual personality—as racer and luxury tourer—was international, thanks to the energetic efforts of Emil Jellinek, the Austro-Hungarian Consul in Nice. He acted as an unofficial agent, selling Daimlers to his friends. The car rightly bore his daughter's name, for it could scarcely have happened without his sizable backing and a firm order for 36 of the new type.

Output of the 5.9-litre, pump-cooled engine, with its twin side camshafts, was 35 bhp at 1,000 rpm, and the drive was transmitted via a four-speed gearbox and scroll clutch to the usual exposed side chains. The frame rode on four semi-elliptic springs, and the foot-brake worked on the transmission; it was kept cool by water from an underfloor-mounted tank. Fuel was fed from a rear tank by exhaust pressure, with an auxiliary hand pump for starting. The car retained sight-feed lubrication, by a battery of oilers on the dash, and the wheels were still of unequal diameter front and rear, which meant that spare tyres had always to be duplicated.

A Mercedes was an expensive plaything. By the time the breed reached Britain in 1902, the improved 40 hp cost £2,000 ($10,000), and a further £800 ($4,000) would be asked for the monstrous 9.2-litre Sixty of 1903. In return for this, the owner had a potential race winner that would outrun anything else on the road. The real problem was, of course, tyre consumption. Top speed of a 35 in road trim was around 50 mph (80 km/h), though Sixties could top the 70 mark.

This badge appeared only on Scania-Vabis products from 1911. It commemorates, however, the chain wheel of Scania bicycles and the eagle emblem of Scania's home city, Malmö.

Scania
1902, Sweden

1902 Scania

Sweden was as yet infertile soil for the new form of locomotion. Roads were poor, and the winter climate savage. Thus Swedish engineers tended to be more interested in commercial vehicles, which had a useful potential as feeders to a scattered railway network. Of the country's three major manufacturers in early days–Scania of Malmö, Vabis of Sodertälje, and Tidaholm–the two former (who merged in 1911) were always better known for their trucks, while Tidaholm made virtually nothing else.

Scania had been founded in 1894 to make British Humber bicycles under licence. Their first experimental cars appeared in 1901, from the drawing-board of Fridolf Thorssin. They were powered by single-cylinder aircooled engines of German Kämper make, set transversely underfloor at the rear. Drive was taken via a two-speed epicyclic gearbox to a central chain.

During 1902, water cooling was tried on a vehicle which conformed, predictably, to the *système Panhard*. Its twin-cylinder engine, still a Kämper product, lived under a frontal bonnet, and the driveline now embraced a three-speed gearbox and side chains. Scania also tried another aircooled unit of Swedish make, though in the 1905–10 period design settled down, with emphasis on conventional watercooled fours, made in very small numbers. Nor did the merger with Vabis lead to any increased interest in private cars: between 1906 and 1924 (when the group finally devoted itself to trucks) a mere 485 were turned out. Until the advent of the Volvo in 1927, Swedes were content to rely on the United States and Germany for their personal transport.

Wolseley 10 hp
1902, Great Britain

Mass production was a long way away in Britain in 1902, when the country's largest maker, Wolseley, had a potential of some 500 cars a year: in 1901 they had delivered 323. The firm, originally makers of sheep-shearing machinery and now owned by the Vickers ordnance empire, had entered the automobile industry in 1895, with the appointment of Herbert Austin to take charge of the new department. From experimental, Bollée-inspired tricars, he had progressed by 1899 to a four-wheeler with horizontal single-cylinder engine, belt primary drive to a three-speed gearbox, and side-chain final drive. This had performed with distinction in the Thousand Miles' Trial of 1900, and series production followed.

Wolseleys were distinguishable by their side-cranking horizontal engines, the twin-cylinder versions being set across the frame. Ignition was by twin coils, and lubrication by drip feeds. The primary belt had, however, been scrapped in favour of a chain, and the gearbox was given four forward speeds. The pressed-steel frame incorporated four cross-members, and as usual the footbrake worked on the transmission. Production Wolseleys unlike the 1899 prototype, had wheel steering.

Certainly the cars were not under-cooled since the radiator area wrapped round the low bonnet, with vertical, interconnected water tanks on either side. The engines were very slow-turning: this 10hp model delivered its maximum power at 700rpm, while the progressive gearchange was also very slow, and modern drivers would be confused by the right-hand clutch pedal. Apart from a tendency to break crankshafts when hard pressed, Wolseleys were, however, very reliable, and reasonably priced. A 5hp single-cylinder two-seater cost £250 ($1,250) and the 10hp tonneau £380 ($1,900).

Further development presented technical problems. While it is possible to mount two cylinders transversely side-by-side, the demand for a four led to the adoption of a horizontally-opposed arrangement on the big-

An early use of a windscreen and fixed top on a 1902 Wolseley.

1902 Wolseley 10hp

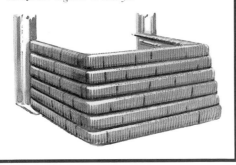

One way of securing an adequate cooling surface was to extend the radiator tubes round the sides of the bonnet, a characteristic of Austin's horizontal-engined Wolseleys.

ger 24hp. In any case, the Mercedes idiom was now in fashion. Wolseley's flat-four racers had a good record, beating the faster Napiers (if not the Continental opposition) in the last two Gordon Bennett Races of 1904 and 1905, but Austin's directors demanded a vertical engine. When he refused to countenance such ideas, they first hired John Davenport Siddeley to design one for them – and then fired Austin. He promptly set up his own company – to manufacture a 25/30hp four with vertical cylinders!

33

CGV 15 hp
1903, France

Fernand Charron, Léonce Girardot, and their partner M. Voigt had all made their names racing for Panhard in the early days. Thus, when they severed their connection with the company and set up in business on their own, it was logical to expect an automobile on Panhard lines.

This was the CGV. Under the bonnet lay a pair-cast, four-cylinder engine with automatic inlet valves and coil ignition. The band-type clutch and four-speed gearbox were also Panhard features, as were the sight-feed lubrication, side-chain final drive, and armoured wood frame. The new car's obvious

The 1902 CGV can be distinguished from a Panhard chiefly by the underslung radiator through which the starting handle projects.

identifying feature was the underslung tubular radiator: Panhards wore their tubes at engine level. Closer inspection revealed that CGV carburetters were water-jacketed, while another refinement was the provision of an auxiliary transverse spring at the rear to smooth out the ride when heavy bodies were fitted.

Sometimes special coachwork assumed extreme forms. While the regular 15 hp CGV measured 92 inches (2.4 m) between axles, Miss Alice de Rothschild commissioned a formidable *diligence* with the passenger compartment entirely separate from the driver's cab, this monster calling for a wheelbase of no less than 150 inches (3.8 m). Another car supplied to an American client in 1906 came complete with lavatory.

Though CGV's racing record never rivalled those of Panhard, Mercedes, or Mors (Girardot's second place in the 1903 *Circuit des Ardennes* was the make's best showing), they had a gearless 8.2-litre straight-eight on the road in 1902, and an impressive list of princely customers for so young a breed. They also built up a useful connection in the United States, where the 15 was marketed at $5,500 (£1,100) inclusive of body. In 1904 came the advent of mechanically operated inlet valves, and by 1906 CGVs were being sold under the Charron name. Later pre-1914 Charrons had dashboard-mounted coolers in the Renault idiom. Conventional radiators would not be seen until after World War I.

1903 CGV 15 hp

Humber
Humberette 5 hp
1903, Great Britain

Two of the Humberette's distinguishing features are the single-spoke steering wheel and the two column-mounted levers for selecting the gears.

By 1903 de Dion-Bouton's inexpensive light cars had been joined by challengers from Peugeot and Darracq, not to mention the miniature Humber illustrated above, the first of its type from a British maker. The light, tubular chassis followed de Dion lines, while the single-cylinder water-cooled 613 cc engine turned at 1,500 rpm, although rotating counter-clockwise, a hazard to unwary crankers.

The Humberette was almost a direct copy of its French prototype. Ignition was by coil, and final drive by shaft and bevel, though the Humber's two-speed gearbox lacked the de Dion's simplicity, being of sliding type and afflicted with two column-mounted levers, for high/low and forward/reverse. The one piece bonnet was of alligator type, and weight was kept to a minimum by the use of aluminium body panels, the elimination of doors and hood, and the cycle-type wire wheels. Doors of a vestigial nature were, however, available for an extra £16 ($80) on the more expensive Beeston version.

For all its 600 lb (275 kg) weight, the car was no brisk performer, attaining only a leisurely 25 mph (40 km/h). It was, however, compact, with an overall length of 94 inches (2.4 m), and even if the catalogue was optimistic in averring that 'all ordinary hills can be taken on the top speed', it met with an enthusiastic reception, 500 finding buyers in the first six months. Better still, it was cheap – at £131 ($655) it was challenged only by the obsolete diamond-pattern Sunbeam-Mabley and the most basic variations-on-a-theme by Lacoste et Battmann (see page 42). A genuine de Dion was priced at £200 ($1,000) and a Wolseley single at £175 ($875). The Post Office tested a delivery van version of the Humberette in London, but a reported thirst of 20 mpg (14 lit/100) suggests that a full load of mailbags was too much for its 5 bhp.

Subsequent models were bigger, the 1905 range including a 7½ hp twin weighing 1,232 lb (560 kg). It had a single-lever gear change and three forward speeds, but retained Humber's single-spoke steering wheel, a hallmark of the breed right up to World War I.

Lanchester 12hp
1903, Great Britain

In the days of Mercedes dominance, the Lanchester might seem to have had a 'horseless' appearance. Almost alone among cars of its period, however, it was designed as an entity, and not just as a chassis to be handed to a coachbuilder capable of inflicting the ultimate in bulk and weight upon it.

Frederick Lanchester and his brother George designed from scratch, without reference to any Panhard ideas. Among the 'firsts' that stand to their credit are a direct drive on top gear in 1896 (an innovation usually ascribed to Louis Renault), silent worm drive, cantilever springs and foot accelerators in 1897, detachable wire wheels and preselective gear change in 1901, and full-pressure lubrication as early as 1904. If true unitary structures lay in the future, the lower part of a Lanchester body was integral with the frame members, giving a structural stiffness seldom encountered in this era. This was further reinforced by the transversely mounted fuel tank, while the unconventional Lanchester-built body was in fact highly practical. On pre-1914 models the engine lived between the front seats, thus saving space and giving excellent forward vision. Dashboard and front wings hinged up to improve access, and the entire rear tonneau of the 1903 car, illustrated below, was detachable, turning it into a two-seater.

Early cars used horizontally-opposed two-cylinder aircooled engines, with mechanically-operated overhead valves: a good balance was assured by the use of two superimposed crankshafts. Ignition was by low-tension magneto, and Lanchester's wick carburetter was dirt-proof. To back up the refinements of the worm drive and cantilever springing, the brothers fitted a crash-proof epicyclic gearbox with central lever control, on the principle of a modern preselector. Even the out-of-date tiller steering was quick, and had the merit that one pointed the lever in the desired direction. By 1903 Lanchester were in process of abandoning the air cooling of early days in favour of a water pump. This apparent concession to orthodoxy in fact added another 2 bhp, hitherto absorbed by the twin fans.

The 1903 12hp car weighed 2,436lb (1,106kg), and attained almost 40mph (65km/h). It was quieter than most of the opposition and consumed fuel at a reasonable 20mpg (14lit/100). Unfortunately, the Lanchesters were constantly beset by commercially-minded directors who demanded that their cars fell into line with rival models. Tiller steering was dropped in 1909 to cope with the growing weight of the latest four- and six-cylinder types. These multi-cylinder units also called for a vertical mounting, albeit still between the front seats. On 1915's Sporting Forty there was even a conventional bonnet, though epicyclic transmission and worm drive survived. Yet as early as 1904, a South African motorist claimed that his Lanchester was the least tiring of all cars, could put 250 miles (400km) into a day's run, and returned 24mpg (12lit/100) even under such conditions.

1903 Lanchester 12hp

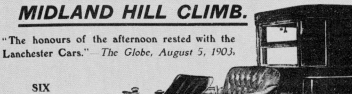

A Lanchester advertisement of 1903 stresses a hill-climb victory but says nothing of the fancy, detachable brougham top, an optional extra.

On the War Office's Lanchesters a different form of weather cover was used: a reversible Victoria top for the officers at the back.

37

An unusual front end: the sloping 'apron' and lack of a conventional bonnet identify pre-1905 Lanchesters.

Oldsmobile Curved Dash Runabout
1903, United States

Henry Ford may have pioneered the moving assembly line, but real mass-production began in 1902 when Ransom Eli Olds turned out 2,500 Curved Dash Runabouts in a year. Thereafter deliveries climbed steadily to their peak of 6,500 units in 1905 before fading away under the influence of more modern designs such as Ford's four-cylinder Model-N.

Olds had realized that a cheap runabout must be simple, and his slogan was 'Nothing to Watch but the Road'. And watching the road was easy, since the Oldsmobile, like the Locomobile steamers it had supplanted, was little more than a buggy with shafts and horse removed, and a power train unobtrusively inserted underneath the structure. Vision was unobstructed. The chassis, too, was pure

buggy: a short frame linked to front and rear axles by quarter-elliptic springs, and reinforced at the front by a transverse full-elliptic arrangement. Steering was by tiller. The horizontal single-cylinder engine lived amidships, delivering its output at a sedate 500 rpm, or 'one chuff per telegraph pole', suitably muffled by an enormous silencer. The two forward ratios of the planetary gearbox were selected by hand: they were also widely spaced, low being very low indeed, and needed even on the gentlest of hills.

The Oldsmobile's leisurely performance on country roads might suggest that it was suitable only as an urban runabout. This was disproved in 1903, when Whitman and Hammond not only drove a Curved Dash Runabout from San Francisco to New York, but managed it in 73 days.

The model survived its production run with little change, though the engine was enlarged and uprated to 7 hp in 1904, and some later versions sprouted dummy bonnets and conventional radiators. Ford had, however, successfully mated a modern four-cylinder power unit to the two-speed transmission in 1906, selling the result for $500 (£100), $50 less than a contemporary Oldsmobile. Thereafter the traditional gas buggies faded away.

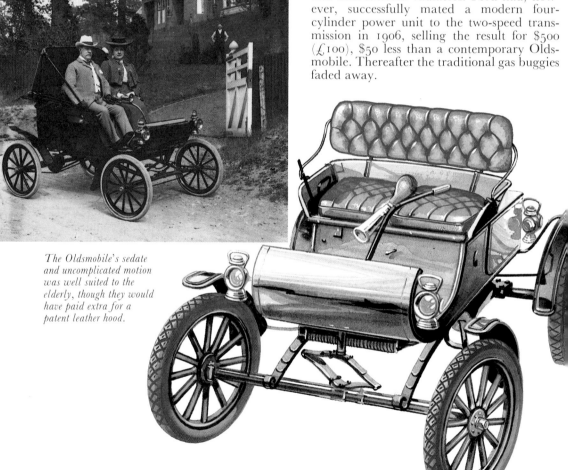

The Oldsmobile's sedate and uncomplicated motion was well suited to the elderly, though they would have paid extra for a patent leather hood.

Daimler 28/36 hp
1904, Great Britain

Daimler of England have long been associated with royalty, funeral corteges, and stately limousines, By contrast, the cars made in the first decade of the 20th century had a marked sporting flavour. Company advertising centred round 'weekly wins' in sprints and hill-climbs: these were recorded in America as well as in Europe.

The 1904 models signalled recovery from shaky finances that had plagued the firm's early years. They also marked the advent of the famous fluted radiator, three-piece alligator bonnet, and such minor distinguishing features as a push-on rather than pull-out handbrake lever and a slatted wooden shield protecting the petrol tank. As all these characteristics survived for many years, it is sometimes difficult to date a Daimler, even though the side-chain drive was dropped after 1908.

In many respects the Daimler followed the established Mercedes theme. Inlet valves were mechanically operated, though British technique was more advanced than German in that Daimler's engineers opted for the single-camshaft L-head type from the start. Coil ignition was standard: magnetos, when fitted, were of the high-tension type. The four-speed selective-shift gearboxes, transmission and rear-wheel brakes, and exhaust pressure fuel feed followed accepted practice. Daimler, however still used tubular radiators, and clung to the old armoured-wood frame until 1906. The 5.7-litre engine's 36 bhp compares closely with the 35 bhp of the slightly bigger 1901 Mercedes, a fact that indicates the German car's *avant-garde* thinking.

'Distinctively different' – even in 1904. This was the first year for Daimler's famous fluted radiator and the legendary three-piece alligator bonnet. The front end would have looked much the same ten years later.

The 1905 competition season proved the Daimler's worth, with six fastest times of the day and seven class wins in Britain alone, not to mention another class victory in the hill-climb section of the German Herkomer Trophy Trials. By 1906, the biggest Daimler ran to a herculean 10.6 litres, and nothing smaller than a 6.8-litre was available. Perhaps unfortunately, the company espoused the Silent Knight sleeve-valve engine in 1908, and though this ensured them a generous share of the chauffeur-driven dowager market, it also meant that half a century would elapse before the world saw another true sports Daimler.

Darracq Flying 15
1904, France

Today we should regard the Flying 15 Darracq as a sports car. A speed of over 45mph (72 km/h) from a touring 3-litre selling in Britain for less than £500 ($2,500) is remarkable when one compares it with the 10hp Wolseley of 1902 (see pages 32–3).

Alexandre Darracq was another graduate from the cycle industry, from which he was bought out in 1896 by a British combine. He then set up in business making cycle components, with brief sallies into electric cabs, rotary-engined motor-cycles, and an unfortunate belt-driven Bollée four-wheeler, before coming up with a more practical shaft-driven lightweight in 1900. This had a tubular frame, 785cc single-cylinder engine, three-speed gearbox, and bevel drive. An unusual feature was the column-mounted gearshift found on most Darracqs up to 1907.

Darracq sold 1,200 units during their first season, subsequently adding a range of twins and fours. These bigger cars had achieved mechanically-operated inlet valves by 1902, while on the Flying 15 there was a further innovation, a one-piece stamped steel frame. Otherwise the car was orthodox, with pair-cast cylinders, and dual ignition with eight plugs. Springs were semi-elliptic at front and rear.

The Flying 15 made its name in long-distance marathons. In America, Darracq importer F. A. La Roche ran his car 2,350 miles (3,760km) in 14 days without stopping the engine, whereupon, on the far side of the Atlantic, Archibald Ford capped his achievement by covering much the same mileage in just over eight days.

Franklin Model-A
1904, United States

Even if design had yet to settle down in 1904, the American Franklin was 'different', with its vertical-four aircooled engine, full-elliptic springing, and liberal use of aluminium—for bodies and differential casings—in pursuit of designer John Wilkinson's passion for weight saving. Later he would use chassis frames of ash, though a subframe of angle iron is still found on the 10hp car illustrated opposite. The engine is set across the frame, Mini-fashion, though the resemblance goes no further, since the drive is transmitted via a two-speed, lever-controlled planetary gearbox and a central chain to the rear axle. Initially, Franklins had only a single contracting band brake on the differential, and the pedal-operated reverse was the official emergency system. By 1904, however, there were two sets of brakes on the rear wheels.

Franklin's slogan 'Scientific light weight' was no idle boast. A two-seater Franklin weighed 1,100lb (500kg), the same as a Curved Dash Oldsmobile and 200lb (90kg) less than a comparable Cadillac, both of them, of course, watercooled. Thus performance was appreciably superior to an Oldsmobile's, as was shown when Whitman and Carris crossed the North American Continent in only 33 days. The Franklin did 40mph (64km/h), and 36mpg (7.9lit/100). Sales in 1904 were an impressive 701 units. From 1905 Franklin began the switch to longitudinal engines, still aircooled.

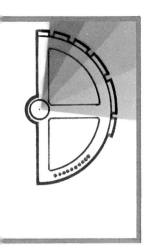

◄ *On a modern steering-column change there are no visible notches on the quadrant, as there are on the 1904 Darracq.*

1904 Kriéger

Kriéger
1904, France

Over the years electric cars changed little, retaining their hippomobile style. Kriéger, their noted French exponent, started his career, like Jacob Lohner, with a line of *avant-train* conversions for horse-drawn carriages. Some of these had electric power steering, more than half a century ahead of the big American manufacturers. A Kriéger taxicab was operating in Paris by the end of 1898. Production models retained front-wheel drive by spur gears, the front axle riding on full-elliptic springs. The two electric motors developed a total of 6 hp, while a goodly proportion of the 3,200-lb (1,400-kg) weight was contributed by the batteries: when Kriéger attempted a 'long-distance' model in 1900, the result was a 2½-tonner. Early models

had wire-rope brakes on the front wheels, which rendered the electric back-up system all the more vital.

In 1904 output was quoted as 9 bhp, and the driver had six forward speeds and two reverses at his disposal. Speed was 15 mph (24 km/h) and range 56 miles (90 km), though a lightweight (760-kg or 1,680-lb) two-seater Electrolette managed 70 miles between recharges.

Kriéger, like Porsche, fell for the attractions of petrol-electrics, listed alongside the standard cars from 1903 onward. The latter could now be had with dummy bonnets (though still with driven front wheels) in 1906. Kriéger battery-electrics were also made under licence in Germany and Italy. In 1908, however, the company was in liquidation.

1904 Franklin Model-A

Horch 18/22 hp
1905, Germany

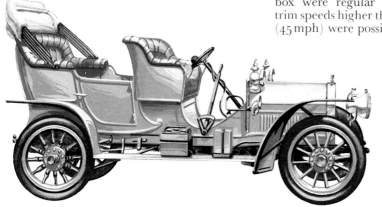

German technical progress was aided and abetted by such long-distance rallies as the Herkomer Trophies (1905–6) and Prince Henry Trials (1907–10). An energetic supporter of such events was August Horch, who built the winner of the 1906 Herkomer, and produced a remarkable streamliner for the 1908 Prince Henry, with dual-cowl four-seater body, cowled radiator, and pontoon running-boards: even the spare tyres were neatly faired into the tail. Horch claimed that these improvements were worth 6bhp in engine performance, but his directors disapproved of money spent on competitions, and fired him a year later.

Horch belonged to a new generation of trained engineers, having been Karl Benz's works manager at Mannheim for three years (1896–9) before setting up on his own. His 2.7-litre four-cylinder 18/22 was typical of its period. Engine speeds were going up, and the car's overhead-inlet-valve unit developed its maximum power at 1,400 rpm. Ignition was by high-tension magneto, and shaft drive had supplanted chains, except on the biggest cars. The leather cone clutch, exhaust pressure fuel feed, pressed steel frame and four-speed gearbox were regular practice. In competition trim speeds higher than the advertised 70 km/h (45 mph) were possible.

This Horch is typical of 1905, though on a high-performance car shaft drive represents advanced thinking. Gear and handbrake levers are mounted together on the right-hand side; there are no front doors; wheels and rims are both non-detachable; and oil and acetylene lamps are used.

Lacoste et Battmann 6 hp
1905, France

One seldom heard of this make outside its native France. Yet a vast and complex range of singles, twins and fours from $4\frac{1}{2}$ to 40 hp was offered. Engines were to customer's choice: the only sure thing was that they were not made by Messrs Lacoste and Battmann!

While suppliers of proprietary components were firmly established in 1905—de Dion and Aster made engines for countless small firms—Lacoste et Battmann went even further. They sold a complete car—to which the nominal maker added paint, trim, and a data plate (radiator badges were not yet in fashion). You had the bonnet you fancied: 'Panhard' or 'Mercedes' styles in early days, giving way later to imitations of Delaunay-Belleville and Gobron-Brillié. The single-cylinder Lacoste runabout featured an armoured-wood chassis with tubular subframe for engine and gearbox, outboard rear springs, and a bevel-drive back axle. The sliding-type gearbox came with two or three forward speeds.

The make had eight certain British aliases in 1904, and could be had in 1905 as an Anglian, Cupelle, Gamage, Jackson, Régal or Speedwell. Gamages might observe piously that their *voiturette* 'cannot be purchased elsewhere under another name', but often a reluctance to spend money on their own advertising illustrations gave the game away. The price of a 6hp two-seater in 1905 could be anything from £130 ($650) to £150 ($750).

1905 Lacoste et Battmann 6 hp

White 15 hp
1905, United States

While the light steam buggies faded from the American scene in about 1904, Rollin H. White's more sophisticated models (with water-tube instead of fire-tube boilers, and instantaneous steam generators of semi-flash type) had a longer run; they accounted for over 9,000 vehicles in the first decade of the 20th century. The first Whites had the reach-bar frames, exposed motion and chain drive of

White Steamers were the official transport of the White House in 1908. Here President Theodore Roosevelt takes the air in a 30hp touring car.

the early Stanley-Locomobile family, though automatic lubrication was used as early as 1901. Wheel steering, and conventional armoured wood chassis riding on semi-elliptic springs, came in 1903. The double-acting compound engine was mounted under a gasoline-type bonnet at the front, though the boiler still lived under the front seat.

Whites were now shaft-driven, looked like gasoline cars even down to frontal 'radiators' (condensers) and could match them on performance, doing 15 mpg (18.8 lit/100) on fuel and 8.3 mpg (about 33 lit/100) on water, with a range between refills of 80–100 miles (130–160 km). Controls followed petrol-car style with brake and pressure pump to the driver's right, though he had also to cope with four pedals (brake, reverse, valve cutoff, and fuel pressure). By 1905, sophistication extended to a free-engine clutch giving a neutral for traffic, and a two-speed rear axle, regarded similarly to the 'low' position on a modern automatic and reserved for exceptionally steep gradients.

Unfortunately, the gasoline revolution was under way. White sales reached their peak in 1906, and though they stayed over 1,000 units a year in ensuing seasons, from 1910 the company switched to petrol-engined luxury cars. After 1918 they abdicated into trucks, which they still make.

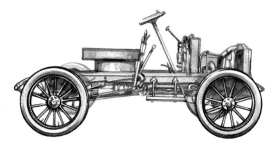

The White chassis was almost conventional in so far as the engine lived under a frontal bonnet, with the condenser taking the place of a petrol car's radiator. The underseat location of the boiler, however, alarmed nervous passengers.

Maxwell Model-L
1906, United States

Jonathan Maxwell had worked with the pioneer Haynes-Apperson concern in Indiana, and thus rated as a second-generation manufacturer. Also second-generation in outlook were his cars, still with horizontal engines, but now featuring shaft drive. Two cylinders replaced the solitary 'pot' of Oldsmobiles and Cadillacs, and the frontal bonnet was no dummy: it wore a Mercedes-style cooler for the thermo-siphon circulation. Inlet valves were mechanically-operated, though the old

States Motor Company, a consortium intended to rival William C. Durant's infant General Motors, its products embracing the inexpensive single-cylinder Brush as well as luxury models (Columbia, Stoddard-Dayton) and trucks (Alden-Sampson). But though 16,000 Maxwells were sold in 1911, the under-capitalized empire was riding for a fall, and in the ensuing bankruptcy only Maxwell lived to fight again. A line of cheap, conventional fours would carry them through to 1925, though the name barely survived a takeover by Walter P. Chrysler. The Maxwell's successors were the 50-series Chrysler (1925–28) and thereafter the Plymouth.

planetary transmission survived: it would be used on twin-cylinder Maxwells to the end of the line in 1912. The channel-section frame and semi-elliptic springing likewise reflected big-car practice, though Model-L still weighed in at around 1,000lb (453kg). It was also cheap: $780 in America, and 165 guineas in England, where it took its first bow in 1906. Top speed was 35mph (56km/h), and catalogues boasted of the 6mph (9.5km/h) available in reverse!

Maxwell sales passed the 2,000 mark for the first time that season, less than two years after the make's debut. The advent of a companion four-cylinder model led to the opening of a new factory at Newcastle, Indiana. In 1910 Maxwell joined the United

Hispano-Suiza 40/50hp
1907, Spain

Poor, politically unstable, and ill-served with roads – the city of Cadiz was still approached by 'seas of mud and ruts' – Spain offered even less promise for motor manufacturers than did Italy. What she did possess was a youthful monarch, Alfonso XIII, who drove himself, and drove fast. Thus royal patronage was accorded to the Hispano-Suiza within a year of the make's inception.

As the name implied, the *marque*'s chief engineer was a Swiss from Geneva, Marc Birkigt, who arrived in Barcelona in 1899. Initially he worked in civil engineering, and then with Emilio La Cuadra's electric-car venture. Petrol-engined prototypes were also made before the money ran out: the same fate attended Birkigt's second backer, a certain Señor Castro, though in the two years of that company's life some advanced four-cylinder machinery with shaft drive and mechanically-operated side-valves in a T-head had been produced.

With healthier finances and the support of Damien Mateu, the Hispano-Suiza firm came into being in June 1904. Over the next two years Birkigt evolved further four-cylinder types based on the defunct Castro. Honey-comb radiators featured, ignition was by high-tension magneto, and Birkigt's gearboxes (like Henry Royce's) had four forward speeds with an overdrive top. The Swiss engineer was also a devotee of the unit box integral with the engine, soon to be general practice. Interestingly, the object of this exercise was not so much simplified production as structural strength. By using the box as a frame member he could cut down on cross bracing.

By 1907, the cars were becoming known outside Spain, with agencies in France and Britain. The 40/50 was a big car of 7.4 litres' capacity, with dual ignition and two plugs per cylinder, capable of 60mph (100km/h). For those demanding still more performance and flexibility there was a huge 11.2-litre six on a 128-inch (3.25m) wheelbase. Better still, royal patronage led to the development of a line of sports cars, and to successful participation in racing. The long-stroke 3.6-litre Alfonso model existed in prototype form in 1907, though the illustrious label itself arrived two years later, when Queen Victoria Eugenie gave her husband a white roadster as a birthday present.

The Hispano-Suiza badge combined the red-and-yellow of Spain with the white cross of designer Birkigt's native Switzerland.

1907 Hispano-Suiza 40/50hp

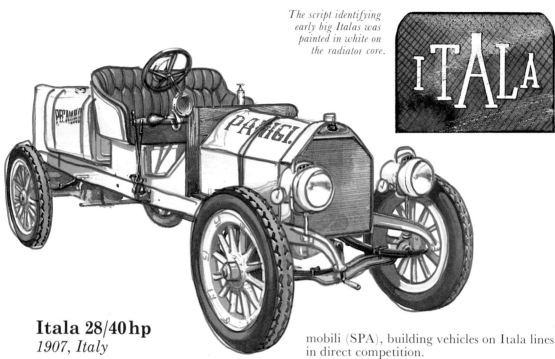

Itala 28/40 hp
1907, Italy

It can hardly be a coincidence that Spain and Italy, two impoverished Catholic countries with negligible home markets, produced two contemporary, rival models, both with 7.4-litre T-head four-cylinder engines, four-speed gearboxes, and shaft drive. Northern Italy had, however, 30 years of successful industrialization behind her, and the country built big and expensive, for such export markets as the the United States and Britain. Fiat, Isotta Fraschini and Itala were already internationally respected in 1907.

The Itala was the creation of Matteo, youngest of the three car-making sons of a watchmaker from Cuneo, Giovanni Ceirano. In 1906 he would move down the road in Turin to found the Società Piemontese Automobili (SPA), building vehicles on Itala lines in direct competition.

Forget the shaft drive, and one encounters the Mercedes theme all over again—a similar four-cylinder engine, low-tension magneto ignition, a gearbox with selective gate change, splash lubrication, and watercooled transmission footbrake (Itala used two of these last!)

Customers included the King and Queen Mother of Italy, though the reigning Pope hated cars and refused to ride in the Itala he was given in 1909. The seal was set on the marque's success with Prince Scipione Borghese's victory in the 1907 Peking-Paris Race, on such a 28/40 loaded to the formidable weight of two tonnes. The car survived 8,000 nearly roadless miles (13,000 km), completing the course with one impoverished wheel run up by a Siberian village wheelwright. No wonder that two British makers (BSA and Weigel) shamelessly cribbed the design.

1907 Laurin-Klement FF

The Laurin-Klement badge.

Laurin-Klement FF
1907, Austria

Pullcar
1907, Great Britain

The straight-eight engine is normally associated with the 1920s. Such a unit (CGV's 1902 effort) did, however, anticipate such pioneer sixes as Napier and Spyker. But while CGV proposed to dispense with a gearbox altogether, Laurin and Klement of Jungbunzlau (now Mlada Boleslav) retained an orthodox four-speed setup.

Initially, the two Austro-Hungarian engineers made bicycles under the Slavia name. In 1898, Vaclav Klement visited France to study the internal-combustion engine. The firm made Werner-type motor-cycles before testing their first car in 1905. Conventional inline fours were available by 1906, and the company soon gained a foothold in Japan, selling the Imperial Army its first motor truck in 1909.

At the 1907 Paris Salon, Laurin-Klement fielded the FF, driven all the way from Jungbunzlau. Engineering was orthodox, with leather cone clutch, pressed steel frame, and bevel-driven back axle. Under the bonnet,

Almost the only early examples of front-wheel drive were *avant-train* conversions of horsed vehicles (see page 27). New in 1906 was J. S. Critchley's British Pullcar, with Mini-style transversely-mounted four-cylinder engine. Primary drive was by chain from a two-speed epicyclic box to a countershaft, whence a roller chain connected with the front axle. Twin transmission brakes were supplemented by whatever anchors came with the horse-drawn carriage-based rear end. Engines were bought elsewhere: the prototype used a 1.4-litre Fafnir, replaced on production models by a slightly more powerful White & Poppe. Pneumatic tyres were furnished for the fore-carriage, which rode on half-elliptic springs.

Early Pullcars had four pedals (low, high, reverse, and the brake) but the 1907 model's extra forward ratio called for a fifth. Though

1907 Pullcar

however, was a power unit of formidable length consisting of two monobloc fours, one behind the other. Each block had its own high-tension magneto.

The problem was crankshaft vibration. The FF's five-bearing crankshaft must have been impossibly whippy, and not everyone was as resourceful as Napier's S. F. Edge, who made a virtue of tooth-shaking 'periods', which he called 'power rattles'. Though Laurin-Klement survived the dismemberment of the Habsburg Empire, emerging in the 1920s as the Czechoslovak Skoda, nothing more was heard of Type-FF.

an elegant C-sprung victoria with canework panelling was exhibited at the 1907 London Show, the makers always regarded their 'car' as a hansom-cab attachment. *The Autocar*'s cautious observation that 'it will be interesting to see when the advantages of this type will be appreciated' had justification. The Pullcar vanished from the market during 1908, a victim of such conventional taxicabs as Unic and Renault. Henceforward the *avant-train* principle was relegated to the motorization (in America) of huge, horsedrawn steam fire engines.

Rolls-Royce 40/50hp
1907, Great Britain

At the beginning of 1907 Charles Stewart Rolls was better known than Frederick Henry Royce – he had, after all, won the previous year's Tourist Trophy on a 20hp Rolls-Royce. The factory was still in Manchester, and total deliveries to date amounted to less than 100 cars, with two, three, four, six and eight cylinders. Of these, the vee-eight was still-born, and the six-cylinder 30 notorious for crankshaft vibration.

Within three years, the *marque* had become a household word in luxury-car circles. The Silver Ghost might possess few revolutionary features. Other breeds (Austro-Daimler, the bigger Hotchkisses) might outpace it. What was recognized was that the six-cylinder 40/50, now the firm's staple product, gave an entirely adequate performance, gave it in smoothness and silence, and would go on giving it after mileages which left rival breeds ripe for the scrap-heap.

The fact that the original Silver Ghost (the name would be applied retrospectively to all side-valve 40/50s) had successfully undergone an officially observed 15,000-mile (24-000-km) trial was significant enough. Troubles were limited to a magneto failure (of little import with dual ignition) and one accidental closure of the petrol tap, and the car averaged 17.8mpg (16lit/100) as well as 2,500 miles (4,000km) per tyre. Little over £2 ($10) was

needed to restore the vehicle to new condition at the end.

Royce was a perfectionist rather than an innovator. The main design features side valves in an L-head, high-tension magneto ignition, cone clutch, four-speed sliding-type gearbox and bevel drive were all well established, though few other makers as yet used full-pressure lubrication, dispensing with the messy sight-feeds. Exhaust pressure fuel feed was of course used on the 1901 Mercedes.

The 40-50 changed relatively little during a long run that ended in 1925. Inevitably the car received the 'period' refinements quick-detachable wheels, electric lights and starter, and eventually four-wheel brakes but major revision was confined to suspension and gearbox, apart from the elimination of the foot-operated transmission brake in 1913. Early cars had a supplementary transverse spring at the rear to eliminate side-sway with towering limousine bodies, this system giving way in due course to longitudinal cantilevers of Lanchester type. In 1909, the demand for silence would kill off the overdrive fourth gear, which offered effortless and surprisingly frugal cruising at 60mph (100km/h) at the price of an irritating whine. At the same time capacity went up to 7.4 litres.

None the less, even the early Ghosts were remarkable cars. A speed of 70mph was attainable with suitably light bodywork, a gallon of petrol lasted 16–18 miles, and a tourer could be bought complete for as little as £1,400 ($7,000), a lot of money compared with £200 runabouts in the de Dion or Rover class, but cheap in relation to foreign imports like the big Benz, Italas, and Lorraine-Dietrichs.

◄Rolls-Royce's emblem was red, and would not change to black until 1933.

A delightfully formal single cabriolet Rolls-Royce built by Barker on a 1912 chassis.

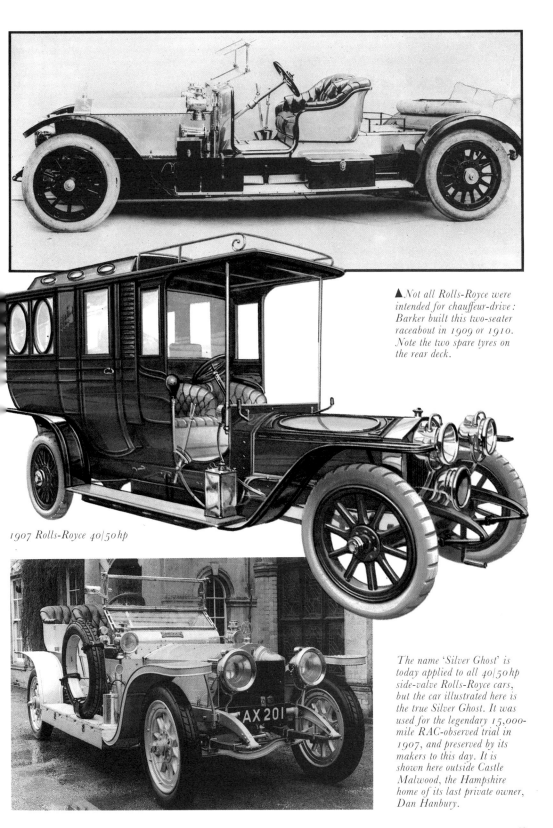

▲ *Not all Rolls-Royce were intended for chauffeur-drive: Barker built this two-seater raceabout in 1909 or 1910. Note the two spare tyres on the rear deck.*

1907 Rolls-Royce 40/50 hp

The name 'Silver Ghost' is today applied to all 40/50 hp side-valve Rolls-Royce cars, but the car illustrated here is the true Silver Ghost. It was used for the legendary 15,000-mile RAC-observed trial in 1907, and preserved by its makers to this day. It is shown here outside Castle Malwood, the Hampshire home of its last private owner, Dan Hanbury.

49

Standard 20 hp
1907, Great Britain

1908 was perhaps the six-cylinder's first banner year, with no fewer than 55 different makes sold on the British market. Not all were large and expensive: the Standard illustrated here, for instance, rode on a compact 116-inch (2.95 m) wheelbase, with a capacity of a mere 3.3 litres as against the 12.9 of the biggest Itala. Better still, it offered a speed range of 2–40 mph (3–60 km/h) in direct drive ('without touching the clutch') for a modest £470 ($2,350). In this price bracket the customer would expect some vibration: the Standard cannot have been too gross an offender, for while many firms soon reverted to fours, its makers had a six continuously in their catalogue from 1905 to 1912.

Their sales were certainly helped by London agent Charles Friswell, who arranged for the despatch of a fleet of 20 hp cars to India in 1911 as official transport at King George V's Delhi Durbar. Nor were all these Standards small cars: while the 1907–8 model had originally been planned as a 1.9-litre to sell for under £300 ($1,500), at the other end of the scale was a huge 11½-litre 50 which made a brief appearance in 1907.

Engineering was conventional, though there were experiments with twin carburetters and air cooling in 1906, and some models had four-speed overdrive gearboxes. Frames were of pressed steel, inswept at the front and upswept at the rear, while the twin camshafts of early types had given way to the L-head configuration. Ignition was by magneto, and power was transmitted via a wet-plate clutch to a three-speed box. A recent innovation was Standard's shouldered radiator shell: this, and the Union Jack badge, would be hallmarks of the breed until 1930.

Turcat-Méry Six-Wheeler
1907, France

'Colonial' models engaged many a maker's attentions. These were recognizable by their bigger wheels, stiffer springs, and raised ground clearance. A more enterprising solution—subsequently applied to military vehicles—was the provision of extra wheels to take the load. This was pursued by Turcat-Méry of Marseilles, who designed cars for Lorraine-Dietrich, and built similar vehicles under their own name.

The vehicle illustrated is the Lorraine-Dietrich version, using the mechanical elements of their 40 hp chain-drive luxury tourer. To this was added an extra dead axle, the four rear wheels being interconnected by pairs of C-springs in series. The centre pair of wheels drove, while additional manoeuvrability was ensured by making the rearmost axle a steerer. This arrangement permitted the six-wheeler to surmount ditches, or even 12-inch logs.

The result was, however, far too unwieldy for a private car. In any case, a puncture-conscious public wanted no part of it: there were too many tyres to change. The idea never caught on, though a demonstrator came to London in 1907, and a magnificent berline was sold to the Khedive of Egypt. A truck version also appeared in that year's French Army vehicle trials.

Six-wheeled private cars like the Turcat-Méry have never caught on, largely because other and better means of smoothing the ride were achieved. Crossley and Morris-Commercial, however, toyed with machines for off-road use in 1928–31, some going to Indian princes as hunting cars.

OTAV 5½hp
1908, Italy

The OTAV of 1908 anticipated the cyclecar boom by some three years. It also ran against the trend of Italian design, since Max Türkheimer, the Milanese cycle maker who backed it, hoped to find a market for a cheap runabout costing a mere one-seventh as much as full-size cars.

The chassis was conventional, apart from the use of quarter-elliptic springs (a recognized money-saver) all round. Front and rear axles were tubular, but the chain-cum-belt drive was far out-of-date, although the use of twin side belts for the final stage marked a reversal of the traditional Benz practice. A simple planetary gear gave two forward speeds, selected by a right-hand lever: no reverse was fitted since this was not required by law in Italy on 200-kilogram lightweights. Equally archaic was the engine, an aircooled single with automatic inlet valve. The 30mph (50km/h) top speed sounds possible, but on Italy's mountainous roads it can never have been the top-gear car it was alleged to be.

More sophisticated small cars were on their way. The OTAV had little export appeal even at bargain prices, and an economic crisis at home was playing havoc with market and industry alike. The make lasted only a year: even a merger with Giovanni Ceirano's Junior (a full size machine) could not save it. Italy would not offer a successful cheap baby car until the advent of the 990cc Fiat 509 in 1924.

The OTAV might be underpowered for Italy and too primitive for most export markets, but in a British trial this example averaged more than 18mph (29km/h) and returned 38mpg (7.5lit/100).

1908 OTAV 5½hp

A Renault completely equipped with hood, windscreen and lamps, though on this car only oil sidelamps are furnished, and there are no doors. The large number of these cars still running attests to their reliability.

Renault 8 hp
1908, France

In 1908, twin-cylinder cars still had a following in the 1-litre class. Right up to World War I a sizable proportion of Renault's output (4,600 units in 1908, over 10,000 in 1913) consisted of their excellent and dependable little twins. There was nothing cyclecar in their make-up: the side-valve engine was half a four, with Renault's proven thermo-siphon cooling and dashboard radiator, the latter doubling as a cockpit heater in winter. Ignition was by high-tension magneto, and the three-speed unit gearbox incorporated a direct top. The clutch was an inverted cone.

The car came in two wheelbase lengths, the longer being well-suited for taxicab work. The legendary *Taxis de la Marne*, in which General Galliéni rushed his troops from Paris to repel von Kluck's armies in 1914, were twin-cylinder Renaults. Top speed was an adequate 35 mph (56 km/h), and the Renault would plod happily along for hours on end at 25–30 mph (40–50 km/h). The only real fault was the progressive gearchange, hard to operate quietly, and retained to the end despite the standardization of the selective gate on other makes. Brakes were the usual rear-wheel and transmission type.

Initially, of course, Renault supplied chassis only, but during 1908 they made a bid in the cheap runabout market with the AX, illustrated above, on an 82½-inch (2.1 m) wheelbase frame and selling in England for £200 ($1,000) complete. 'Complete' was, of course, a relative term. There were no doors, and lamps and hood were extra!

Thomas Flyer 50 hp
1908, United States

From 1904 American industry concentrated more and more on bigger cars. These were constructed on European lines, and often designed by European engineers, too. Gustave Chedru from Clément-Bayard, and M. A. Longeron and Charles Muller (from Mors) worked for Thomas.

Erwin Ross Thomas had started as a bicycle manufacturer in Cleveland, Ohio. From there he moved to Buffalo, where he built motorcycles and light runabouts. The latter differed from other 'gas buggies' in having three-speed sliding-type gearboxes. The company's first 'European' models were, curiously, vertical-threes, the four-cylinder line beginning in 1904 with a 40 hp credited with 4–60 mph (6–100 km/h) in top. This followed Mercedes lines, with pair-cast cylinders, side valves in a T-head, steel frame, and side-chain drive, though early examples had quadrant change, and magneto ignition was not adopted until 1906. By this time Thomas had delivered over 1,000 large cars. In 1907 they opened a branch factory in Detroit to build smaller shaft-drive fours. This did not prosper, and was soon sold to Chalmers.

In 1908 came the Thomas's victory in the New York-Paris Race, while the company was supplementing its fours with a line of sixes headed by the enormous 12.8-litre K6-70, guaranteed to do 72 mph (115 km/h). Thereafter Thomas slid quietly downhill: the factory was sold up in 1913, despite a claim that 6,000 of the 7,000 cars built to date were still running.

Vauxhall 20 hp
1908, Great Britain

Even as late as 1925 Britain's Vauxhall proudly bore the slogan: 'The Car Super-excellent', and was rated among the world's

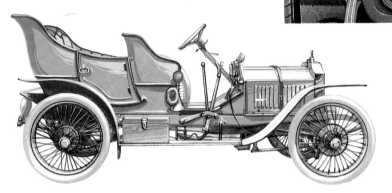

Although early Vauxhalls had only vestigial flutes confined to the bonnet top, by 1908 these had become an identifying feature. They were still to be seen as late as 1962.

finest fast tourers. Yet Laurence Pomeroy's first design was almost an accident of birth.

The former marine-engine works' first cars had been single-sylinder 'gas buggies' in the American idiom, noted for their all-coil spring-ing and the flutes on the bonnet top, trans-ferred to the radiator on later vertical fours. There had been some curious experiments, such as an inline three with six forward speeds, and a powered hansom cab in which the driver sat above and behind his fare. Had chief engineer F. W. Hodges not gone on holiday in Egypt shortly before the Royal Automobile Club's 1908 2,000-Mile Trial, the 20 might never have happened.

Pomeroy's chassis was conventional enough, with its half-elliptic springs and transmission-cum-rear-wheel brakes (the make's Achilles' Heel in post 1918 days). Where he scored was in his engine, an advanced affair designed for high rates of rotation. It achieved its 38 bhp at

a then alarming 2,000 rpm, thanks to efficient gas flow, full-pressure lubrication, and a robust five-bearing crankshaft. Cooling was by thermo-siphon, a cone clutch was used, and in the Trial the car was the best overall performer. It proved capable of 55 mph (90 km/h) with an overall thirst of 26 mpg (10.8 lit/100). By 1910, a direct development, the Prince Henry sports model, offered 60 bhp, and 1914's 4-litre versions were good for 75–80 mph (120–130 km/h).

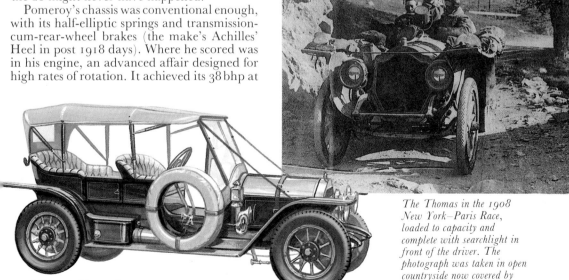

1908 Thomas Flyer 50 hp

The Thomas in the 1908 New York–Paris Race, loaded to capacity and complete with searchlight in front of the driver. The photograph was taken in open countryside now covered by Greater Los Angeles.

Ford Model-T
1909, United States

The Universal Car's achievements still astonish, even 70 years after its introduction. Its overall sales record during an 18-year run (over 16 million units) has been beaten only by the Volkswagen Beetle—and this car took over 30 years to do it. It brought motoring to the masses, while its descendants, the TT commercial (1917) and the Fordson tractor (1916) had the same effect on trucking and mechanized agriculture respectively. At peak in 1923, annual production came close to the two million mark. It was the model that popularized left-hand steering in America, while the need to make still more Ts led to the introduction of the moving assembly line.

When it first appeared, no one had ventured a full four-seater with a four-cylinder engine at less than $1,000 (£200). Its detachable cylinder head, a prime aid to servicing, was distrusted by many engineers, Henry Royce

included, since early gaskets did not seal well. Towards the end, of course, the Ford became a joke: two-speed planetary transmissions were outmoded by 1912 and peculiar to the breed by 1918, while the car's indifferent two-wheel brakes and archaic non-styling had no place amid the sophistication of 1927. The public wanted bright colours, not the unrelieved black affected by Ford for so many years. Even if parts could be bought in every country store, the 'Tin Lizzie' had had its day.

Not so in 1909. Already established as America's best-selling maker with a $500 (£100) runabout, Ford now offered still more for $850 (£170). The slow-turning 2.9-litre four-cylinder engine gave a speed of 40 mph (64 km/h). The combination of transverse-leaf springing and a high ground clearance made it ideal for countries with bad, or non-existent roads. Further, the three-pedal layout adopted was proof against any combination of ignorance and panic, since whichever pedal one trod upon, it would at least retard the car's progress. The wide gap between high and low

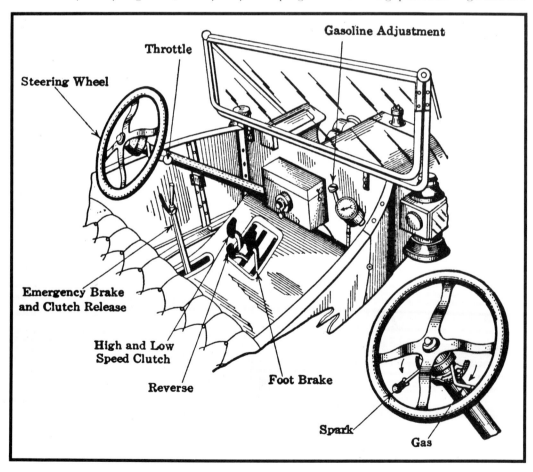

◀ *The foolproof motor-car at last, and the first car to popularize left-hand drive, if not its pioneer. The only lever is the handbrake; the three pedals, left to right, engaged low gear (which slowed the car effectively), reverse (the most dramatic method of stopping) and the footbrake (not very efficient). There were no instruments at all.*

▶ *The first Model-T touring cars were usually doorless. Front doors were not added until 1912.*

reduced the speed to 15mph (24km/h), the foot transmission brake did much the same, only less effectively, and the ultimate braking resource was reverse, also useful for the steepest hills (and on lesser ones when one was short of fuel!)

There were also idiosyncrasies. Cold starting was best undertaken with a rear wheel jacked up: otherwise gummed-up clutch plates helped one to crank the whole transmission, and risk being run over. Starters, available by 1919, were not compulsory until 1926. Another future delight was magneto-driven electric lighting: this gave a brilliant glare when the engine was revving hard, but a feeble glow when one was cruising fast in high gear.

But Model-T was outstanding by any standards. No wonder that over 300,000 found buyers in the last year before World War I, or that ultimately the cars would be made or assembled in Australia, Britain, Canada and France as well as in their native United States.

Martini 10hp
1909, Switzerland

Like the Vauxhall, Charles Baehni's 1909 Martini *voiturette* was an ancestor of the modern sports car. His miniature had been designed for the 1908 *Grand Prix des Voiturettes*. Once again we encounter a neat monobloc four-cylinder engine, albeit with only three main bearings and semi-pressure lubrication. Surprising at so early a date is the shaft-driven overhead camshaft, while fours are still uncommon in the 1,100cc class, where de Dion Bouton are content with one cylinder and Renault with two.

In other respects, the car is conventional enough, with magneto ignition, thermo-siphon cooling assisted by a vaned flywheel, and a pressed steel frame. A separate sub-chassis is retained for the engine and three-speed gearbox, and exhaust pressure feed is not usually found on light cars.

Switzerland was still no nation of motorists. As late as 1913, the country registered less than

5,000 private cars. Martini themselves had led a chequered career. Famed for their repeater rifle, they had made a petrol engine as early as 1887, and were experimenting with complete cars by 1897, though when deliveries began five years later, the product was a licence-built Rochet-Schneider, itself a copy of the Mercedes. From 1904 to 1906, the firm had been under British control. Though 1909 was a good year, with 260 cars sold, the sporting little overhead-camshaft two-seater was short-lived. By mid-1910 the advanced engine had given way to a 1.4-litre side-valve.

1909 Metz

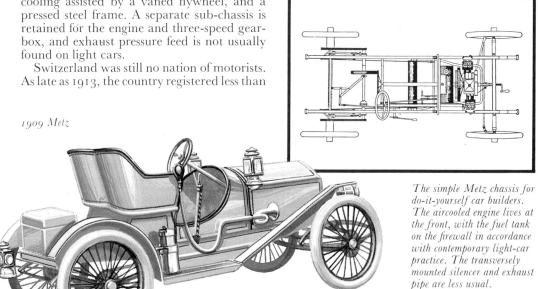

The simple Metz chassis for do-it-yourself car builders. The aircooled engine lives at the front, with the fuel tank on the firewall in accordance with contemporary light-car practice. The transversely mounted silencer and exhaust pipe are less usual.

Metz
1909, United States

Those who regard the kit-car as a tax-dodging device of the 1950s and 1960s may be surprised to discover that an American firm sold no fewer than 6,000 such kits in the 1909–11 period. Under the Metz plan, the customer received his car in 14 successive packages. These started with frame elements and a set of tools, and ended with tank, carburetter, silencer, lamps, horn and starting handle. Each package cost $27 (£4.40), and terms were cash on the nail.

The idea was devised by Charles H. Metz to put the insolvent Waltham Manufacturing Company back on a paying basis. The scheme cleared the inventory of obsolete parts, and was self-financing. There were, of course,

An aircooled car had no radiator to carry a badge, so Sears used old-fashioned brass script. Cars were a short-lived line for this nationally famous mail-order house.

problems. Metz designed the car as he went along, and sometimes more adroit customers got ahead of him. Several of the later packages sold below cost, and though the scheme was launched in the summer of 1908, the first complete kits had not been delivered before October, 1909.

The specification embraced a 10hp aircooled flat-twin engine, an infinitely variable gear, full-elliptic springs, cycle-type wire wheels, bicycle-style brakes at the rear, and a stark two-seater body panelled in aluminium. No hood or windscreen was provided. By 1911 the fortunes of the company were safely restored, and Metz, encouraged by the success of his latest four-cylinder design in the Glidden Tour, offered this only in complete form, still with friction drive. Production reached its peak in 1915, with 7,230 Metzes delivered.

Sears Autobuggy
1909, United States

The short vogue of the high-wheeler was largely confined to America's Middle West. Between 1907 and 1912 perhaps 100,000 were built: at peak, in 1909, 41 different makes were on the market.

Here was a motorized buggy for the farmer, with piano box body, full-elliptic springs, and horse-carriage wheels of generous diameter with solid tyres. This not only resulted in good ground clearance and light weight (the latter important if one ditched the vehicle), but rendered manufacture simple. The vast buggy industry supplied all but the mechanical elements. These were a slow-turning aircooled flat-twin engine, and a simple friction or planetary drive. No more than two speeds

1909 Sears Autobuggy

were required, since hills were few and far between. Tiller steering was general practice. Such a vehicle was cheap: a 1909 Sears retailed for $395 (£79).

The celebrated Sears Roebuck mail order house accounted for some 3,500 units, all sold complete with 32-page instruction manual. A Sears, they said, would 'do anything that a $5,000 car will do, except travel faster than 25 miles an hour'. It was 'up with the chickens, knows no quitting time, and after a day's work is ready for a pleasure trip in the evening'. So, of course, was a Ford, backed by cheap parts and service, and twice as quick. Sears quietly dropped complete automobiles from their catalogues after 1912.

Sheffield-Simplex 45 hp
1909, Great Britain

By 1909 the automobile worked admirably: at least, expensive ones did. Owners with 'motor servants' need never bother themselves with the chores of polishing brass and keeping paint-and-varnish pristine. Tyres, of course, were still a cross to be borne, but the major remaining problem was shifting gears. And since synchromesh lay well in the future, the best palliative was a car that would do 90 per cent of its work in top.

Planetary transmissions were a partial cure, though on these 'low' was very low and still called for frequent use. Six-cylinder engines

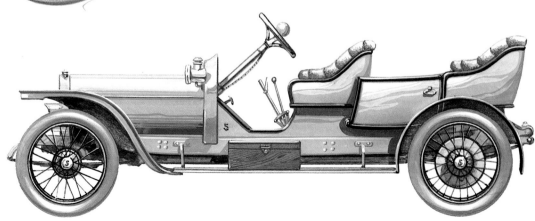

The entwined 'S' badge of Sheffield-Simplex took a leaf out of Rolls-Royce's book. The company also conducted a formidable testing programme in Scotland and the Pennines.

made for greater flexibility, but even with these most makers retained three- and four-speed gear-sets, just to be on the safe side. Not so Earl Fitzwilliam's Sheffield-Simplex company, which advertised a 45 hp 'gearboxless' car in 1909, with pictures of the prototype scaling the toughest passes of its native Yorkshire.

The company had acquired the rights of the four-cylinder Brotherhood car, after its makers had moved from London to Peterborough and lost interest in such activities. Thereafter, fours gave way to an elegant 7-litre six (its cylinder dimensions of 114.3 × 114.3 mm were identical to those of the 40–50 Rolls-Royce. There were other similarities, though Sheffield-Simplex did not use full-pressure lubrication, preferred three speeds to four, combined the footbrake and clutch, and used an accelerator pedal with lateral travel, which last must have confused not a few drivers! The round radiator was a distinguishing feature, and a tourer cost only £855 ($4,275).

The 'gearboxless' 45 (Type LA2) was not, of course, a one-gear car. Instead, the conventional arrangements gave way to a two-speed transaxle alleged to save 150 parts and 300 lb (136 kg). Detachable wire wheels were standardized, and the car would, of course, 'climb anything in top'. Sheffield-Simplex had sufficient confidence in their product to furnish one for the Prince of Wales's West country tour. An officially observed trial showed a 3–60 mph (5–100 km/h) range in top, while use of low when accelerating from rest to 30 mph (50 km/h) saved less than half a second. But though the transaxle survived on Sheffield-Simplexes to the end of production in 1915, 1913 and later models all came with three speeds. And also, be it said, with orthodox accelerator pedals!

Stanley 10 and 20 hp
1909, United States

If White and other steam-car makers (such as Miesse in Belgium) were deserting their first love, the Stanley brothers, back in control of their company since 1902, were irrevocably wedded to the system. Stanley steam cars would be made until 1926, though their 1909 offering was now outwardly conventional, apart from the coffin nose housing the vertical, multi-tubular boiler. Unlike Whites, Stanleys had no condenser, in spite of which the 26-gallon (130-litre) water tank gave a useful range of 50 miles (80 km).

Simplicity remained the keynote. The car's double-acting, simple, twin-horizontal cylinder engine was mounted at the rear with the crankshaft engaging directly on the differential, eliminating the complexities of gears or chains. Steering was of course by wheel, and the wooden chassis rode on full-elliptic springs. The footbrake incorporated a ratchet for parking, while the provision of oil-bath lubrication for the engine simplified maintenance still further.

A paraffin burner was now used, a great improvement on the infuriating firing-iron of Locomobile days, and acetylene lighting systems such as the Prestolite could be adapted to preheat the vaporizer. But there was still the problem of the 25–30 minutes needed to raise steam from dead cold, even if the steam car's habits were essentially more predictable than those of internal-combustion types. The silence of a Stanley engine was offset by an irritating whistle from the burner.

As for the neck snapping acceleration, this was undoubtedly available. Frank Marriott had, after all, attained 127.66 mph (204.25 km/h) at Daytona Beach in 1906 in a Stanley racer, and the cars could be 'rodded' by putting a big-capacity 20 hp boiler in the short '10 hp' chassis. A Stanley was good for 50 mph (80 km/h) and could get there far faster than any stock petrol car, but after a short burst one ran out of steam. The comfortable cruising speed remained 30 mph (50 km/h).

Le Zébre 5CV
1910, France

There are always advocates of basic motoring, which should not be confused with the crudities of the cyclecar. One such advocate was Jules Salomon, better known for the Citroëns of the early 1920s, whose Le Zèbre appeared on the motoring scene in 1910. By this time, of course, really small four-cylinder engines were beginning to make an impact.

Here was a conventional motor-car in miniature with a proper pressed-steel frame, sprung at each corner. The driveline consisted of a sliding-type gearbox (admittedly with only two forward speeds), a disc clutch, and a straight bevel back axle, while the car was more 'modern' than many of its contemporaries in that the footbrake worked on the rear wheels, and not on the transmission. In two respects only was the Le Zèbre unusual: its reversion to a single-cylinder engine, and the use of single-seater bodywork, with a central steering column. This arrangement, however,

was short-lived: almost all production Zèbres were orthodox two-seaters.

Fuel and oil tanks were streamlined into the firewall, and the 7 bhp developed by the 600 cc engine offered a speed of 30 mph (50 km/h), thanks to a weight of only 560 lb (200 kg). A fuel consumption of 50 mpg (5.5 lit/100) permitted a reasonable range even with a two-gallon tank. In France, if not in England, the vehicle sold for the equivalent of £100 ($500). It was still listed in 1914, albeit with a 645 cc engine and three forward speeds.

Singles, however, are rough and can kick viciously if carelessly cranked. De Dion dropped their single-cylinder cars after 1912, and their twins a year later, while such baby fours as the French Charron and Peugeot (see page 80), the German Adler K and the British Singer, were already available. In 1913, Le Zèbre, too, offered a four-cylinder car, this becoming their staple when production was resumed after World War I.

Minerva 16hp
1910, Belgium

If Minerva were not Belgium's first car makers, they were certainly her most famous. Sylvain de Jong of Antwerp started with bicycles, progressing to motor-cycles and proprietary engines for these: among well-known manufacturers to purchase such units were Adler, Enfield, Humber and Opel. Car production began in earnest in 1903, and by 1907 the firm offered two shaft-drive types, a 4.1-litre four and a 6.2-litre six. The latter was good for 60mph on an output of 60bhp.

The year 1909, however, had seen the adoption of the Silent Knight double-sleeve-valve engine. This had its advantages. It 'improved with use', and so seldom needed decarbonizing: 25,000 mile (40,000km) intervals between overhauls were common. On the debit side, it was expensive to make, seizures could be catastrophic, and its thirst for oil was proclaimed by its smoky exhaust. Like Daimler, Minerva plunged whole-heartedly into the new design, and by 1910 the earlier T- and L-head types had given way to a range of Knight-engined fours, capacities being 2.3, 4.2 and 6.3 litres respectively. All had cone clutches, four-speed gearboxes, dual ignition, and the usual transmission and rear-wheel brakes. Detachable wire wheels were standardized from 1911, and the small 16hp, illustrated below, had a detachable cylinder head.

Though a favourite of the aristocracy (Belgium's own King Albert headed the list of royal clients), the 'Goddess of Automobiles' was no sluggard. Big Minervas managed an easy 60mph (100km/h), even with formal bodywork, while the make was twice victorious in the tough Swedish Winter Trials–in 1911 and again in 1914. There were also good performances in the Austrian Alpine event. The 1911 catalogue contained a standardized landaulette body on the 16hp chassis, selling for a modest £595 ($2,980) in England.

Unfortunately, the Belgian industry had always concentrated on expensive cars for export, leaving the domestic cheap-car market open to France and America. An increasingly chauffeur-driven image would render the *marque* one of the first victims of the Great Depression. Minerva hung on until 1936, however, before merging with Imperia, the only other survivor from a once-proud line-up of manufacturers.

Appropriately, Minerva's emblem was the Roman goddess of the same name, and their slogan 'the Goddess of Automobiles'.

Napier 45 hp
1910, Great Britain

In the first decade of the 20th century, the Napier was certainly the most respected British make. The 'first to wear the green' and represent their country in international racing, they had won the 1902 Gordon Bennett Cup. When Germany and France shared the technical leadership between them, Napier–even if they had not invented the six-cylinder engine–could legitimately claim that they were the most consistent of its protagonists, marketing the type without a break, the war years apart, from 1904 to 1924. (Their great publicist S. F. Edge made immense capital out of this.)

A six-cylinder Napier took the world's first 24-hour record at Brooklands in 1907, and Edge never missed out on any stunt that might enhance the car's reputation. As early as 1906, a 60 was submitted to a 1,000-mile (1,600 km) observed top-gear trial, and in 1910 Arthur Macdonald drove a six-cylinder car from London to Edinburgh without a downward shift, turning in 19.35 mpg (14.7 lit/100). Britain's prevailing 20 mph (32 km/h) limit precluded any mention of his average speed, but he subsequently did a Brooklands lap at 76.35 mph (122.18 km/h) leaving the Napier's performance in no doubt. Napiers were made under licence in Italy; American manufacture was also planned, but scarcely began.

The catalogued six-cylinder range of 1910 featured pair-cast, L-head engines with pump and fan cooling and dual ignition. Fuel feed was by exhaust pressure from a rear tank, and the semi-elliptic rear suspension was supplemented by a transverse leaf spring. Standard wheelbase was 134 inches (3.42 m), this chassis coming with two sizes of engine, the 6.2-litre 45 and the 9.7 litre 60; an even larger 90 hp unit was also available. Wire wheels were usually fitted, and the breed's distinguishing features were the forward mounted radiator and its tall 'water tower' filler cap. The smaller 45 was good for over 60 mph (100 km/h), and Edge shrugged the roughness of the unbalanced crankshaft away as the 'power rattle'.

Though Napier finally abdicated from

Napier's first six-cylinder racing car, built in 1904, is here seen contesting the 1905 British Gordon Bennett eliminating trials. It did not do well in the race, however, as its two-speed gearbox could not cope with the steep gradients of the course.

A Napier for a Maharajah, with an engine rated at 120 hp. The extended chassis gave a length of 21 feet (6.5 m), and there was room for 11 passengers.

1910 Napier 45 hp

The front end of a 1914 Napier, showing the make's tall 'water tower' radiator cap.

racing in 1908, sales remained good, reaching a peak in 1911 with 801 cars delivered. The company, however, suffered (like Daimler in later years) from a divided image. Edge might seek to promote the big and luxurious sixes, so much so that his 1908 Tourist Trophy fours were badged and entered as Huttons—but the factory's bread-and-butter came from smaller fours and, worse still, from twin-cylinder taxicabs, a profitable line for several years. (Between 1909 and 1913 nearly 1,500 cabs left the Acton works.) Moreover, well-heeled clients did not like the sight of that aristocratic water-tower on the cabs they hailed in Pall Mall. Edge's resignation in 1913 took much of the fire out of the publicity side, and though a one-model policy (with an ohc six) was pursued after 1918, by this time Napier were pinning their faith solely on aero engines. The last cars were delivered in 1924.

Phänomobil

The most perfect car technically, the most economical in use.

Light, solid, furnished with excellent springs, comfortable, easy to :: operate ::

The car for hilly and :: bad roads ::

Phänomen-Werke
Zittau, Saxony.

In four-cylinder form, the Phänomobil was offered as a four-seater. It might be 'the most perfect car technically', but its appearance was strange, and the steering must have been perilous.

Phänomobil
4/6 hp
1910, Germany

In 1910 heterodoxy still had its strongholds, and among the longer-lived oddities were Germany's three-wheeled Cyklons and Phänomobils, the latter breed enjoying a 20-year run, from 1907 to 1927. It even made its way, albeit anonymously, into popular fiction: Richard Hannay, John Buchan's hero, stole one while engaged on espionage in wartime Germany. His was a light van as used by the postal services, and the device was very popular in commercial form – but either way the principle was the same.

The entire power pack was concentrated at the front; it consisted of a fan-cooled vee-twin engine mounted fore-and-aft over a single wheel with coil-sprung front fork. This was driven via a friction-and-chain gear giving two forward speeds and a reverse. Gears were selected by up and down movement of the steering tiller, which also housed the ignition and throttle levers – one of the few genuine cases of single-lever control! The fuel tank perched perilously on the steering head, while the dead rear axle carried contracting brakes and rode on orthodox semi-elliptic springs. On an output of 7 bhp the light two-seaters (220 kg, or 485 lb) had a top speed of 40 mph (64 km/h). In 1912 a transversely-mounted $1\frac{1}{2}$-litre four (still aircooled) supplanted the twin, and wheelbase was lengthened from 78 inches (1.95 m) to 101 inches (2.56 m), thus permitting full four-seater coachwork. With a conventional tourer body the Phänomobil's appearance was odd in the extreme.

Phänomen-Werke also made conventional cars with watercooled engines. When private-car production ceased, they switched to light trucks using an enlarged development of the original aircooled four, although with shaft-driven rear wheels. Descendants of these were still being produced in the same factory at Zittau by the nationalized East German industry in 1980. Curiously, another Saxon firm, Framo of Hainichen, would revive the Phänomobil theme on a 197 cc cyclecar in 1931/2.

Spyker Twin-Cylinder
1910, The Netherlands

Until the introduction of Van Doorne's belt drive DAF in 1958, Spyker had always been regarded as synonymous with the Dutch car industry, though in fact in 1910 three other firms (Eysink, Omnia and Simplex) were also active. None of these, however, was much known outside Holland, although Eysink's motor-cycles enjoyed an international following.

The Spijker family (a simplified spelling was always used for the cars) were old-established coachbuilders, responsible for the famous Gold Coach of the House of Orange. From 1895 they imported Benz cars, incorporating their own improvements. The next step was to hire a French designer, Émile Drouard, and to launch out on their own with a line of shaft-drive types with two- and four-cylinder T-head engines, noted for their comprehensive undershields. These earned them the sobriquet of the 'Dustless Spykers'. Other early ventures included a strange, boiler-shaped engine designed to give optimum water circulation (it boiled furiously), and a four-wheel drive six in 1904.

Unfortunately, Hendrijk Spijker, the more cautious of the two brothers, died in the wreck of the SS *Berlin* in 1907. The ensuing re-organization brought in a new designer, Valentin Laviolette. He evolved a range of four-cylinder cars with T-head engines and worm-driven transverse camshafts, an unusual arrangement which worked very well. Otherwise his Spykers were orthodox, with thermo-siphon cooling, plate clutches, and three- or four-speed gearboxes (the former on the smaller cars). Capacities ranged from 1.8 up to 7.2 litres, and there was even a four-wheel brake option in 1911. Among the customers was Queen Wilhelmina, who bought three Spykers between 1911 and 1914.

The twin-cylinder runabout illustrated below never passed the prototype stage. A scaled-down edition of the small four, with semi-elliptic springing all round, it suffered a spectacular crash on test, which wrote the first example off. The second, complete with Stepney wheel, was abandoned in a corner of the factory, and has never run under its own power. It now rests in Holland's Nationaal Automobielmuseum at Leidschendam.

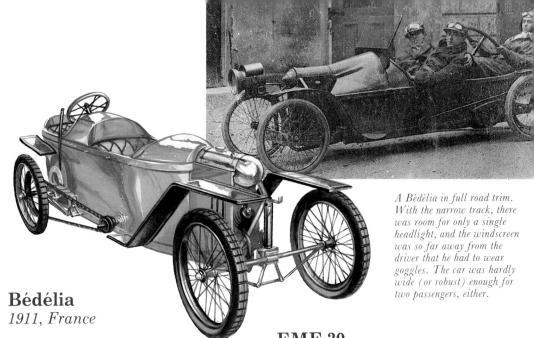

A Bédélia in full road trim. With the narrow track, there was room for only a single headlight, and the windscreen was so far away from the driver that he had to wear goggles. The car was hardly wide (or robust) enough for two passengers, either.

Bédélia
1911, France

If Henry Ford offered the most for the least money, it could be said of the cyclecar that at best it offered sociable accommodation for one graduate motor-cyclist and a friend, while at worst it presented the maximum degree of discomfort the customer could be persuaded to accept.

The French Bédélia was not even sociable: its crew sat in tandem, with the driver behind, as on an 1896 Bollée. The main structure consisted of four ash longerons, with aluminium side panels and a wooden floor. Wheels were of cycle type, and the vehicle combined a centre-pivoting front axle with cable-and-bobbin steering. Engines were of aircooled motor-cycle type: either a proprietary single by Quentin or Bédélia's own vee-twin with automatic inlet valves. In the best motor-cycle tradition, the fuel tank lived atop this unit. The transmission likewise recalled the Bollée: a primary belt to the mainshaft, whence the power was delivered to the wheels by two long side belts. There was no differential, and 'gears' were changed by slackening the motor lugs to move the axle forward in relation to the transmission.

The Bédélia had one major asset: it was very light – 335 lb (150 kg) with the twin-cylinder engine. It could also be bought for less than £50 ($250) in France, though the lowest figure quoted in England was £62 ($310), raised to £94 ($470) by the end of 1911, when both 50 mph (80 km/h) and 50 mpg (5.5 lit/100) were claimed. Remarkably, the cars were still available in 1925, though by this time tandem seating had been abandoned.

EMF 30
1911, United States

One of the forerunners of the Studebaker, the EMF was marketed by that company, and made for them by Everitt-Metzger-Flanders. A cut above Ford and Overland, it sold in the $1,100–1,250 (£220–250) bracket: the same factory's humbler Flanders cost $800 (£160).

In this price class, even in 1909, one expected a proper three-speed, sliding-type gearbox, though the makers mounted it in unit with the back axle, never a very healthy idea. For the rest, the car was orthodox, with a pair-cast four-cylinder engine, magneto ignition, splash lubrication, and cone clutch. The full-elliptic rear springs were designed to cope with America's bad roads, while no transmission brake was fitted: Americans disliked them. The fixed wood wheels wore demountable rims, and the standard colour was blue, with cream running gear.

On paper, the EMF's 50 mph (80 km/h) top speed and 22 mpg (12.5 lit/100) sounded attractive for a 3.7-litre car, but it was dogged by trouble. The first thermo-siphon cooled engines boiled furiously, so a pump was hurriedly substituted. The unreliability of the transaxle earned the car such sobriquets as 'Every Mechanical Fault' and 'Every Morning Fix It'. In spite of this, the combined EMF and Flanders sales climbed steadily, from 7,960 in 1909 to a peak of just over 29,000 in 1912.

For 1913 the EMF and Flanders names were dropped, and the range marketed as Studebakers. The transaxle, however, had several more years to run.

Métallurgique 26 hp
1911, Belgium

When fitted with coachwork by Vanden Plas of Brussels, the Belgian Métallurgique was one of the most beautiful cars of its period. There were such creations as a chariot-style limousine with imitation venetian blinds to the rear quarters, and a 'lounge saloon' for the owner driver with interior electric light. One closed car was given the full Louis XVI treatment, down to Venetian lace headrests and a cupola-style roof. The elegance was completed by the rounded-vee radiator, which set the fashion for a whole generation of sporting cars in Germany. The influence was not surprising: Métallurgiques were designed by a German, Ernst Lehmann, and they were also made under licence in Berlin by Bergmann.

This beauty was more than skin-deep, for Métallurgiques had a well-substantiated reputation for performance. In 1908 their 60/80 hp four (they never made a six) with overhead inlet valves disposed of 86 bhp, and though the side-valve models were less spectacular, the 26, illustrated below, was no sluggard, doing 80 mph (128 km/h) in open form on an output of 60 bhp from 4.9 litres. Specification was close to the period's norm, with pair-cast cylinders, side valves in an L-head, and magneto ignition. The gearbox offered four speeds, and rear springs were three-quarter elliptic. Wire wheels and polished aluminium bonnets were standard equipment, and by 1914 Métallurgique sold their chassis with a two-year guarantee.

War damage and the gradual failure of the all-important British market, however, took their toll, and these former makers of railway equipment built their last car in 1927.

The Métallurgique in classic form, 1914: an interior-drive saloon body with low-pressure tyres to smooth the ride.

1911 Métallurgique 26 hp

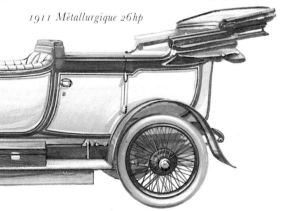

Stoewer B6
1911, Germany

Before 1914 local makes could survive on local sales – in the bigger countries. Of such a stamp was the Stoewer from Stettin in Pomerania, though Émile Mathis's Strasbourg-based agency introduced the breed to Western Germans; it also allowed Mathis to put his own badge on some Stoewers! Export sales were surprisingly good, accounting for some 50 per cent of total production, and extending as far afield as Australia. Annual production, however, seldom passed the 2,000 mark even in the prosperous mid-thirties.

The brothers Bernhard and Emil Stoewer

started by making bicycles in the family iron-works, progressing to motor-cycles and tri-cycles of de Dion type by 1897. These were followed by chain-drive cars in the Panhard idiom (1901) and mock-Mercedes from 1902 onward. The imitative phase was, however, nearly over. Shaft-drive cars were first seen in 1904, and three years later chains had gone for good. In their place came some interesting and individual designs.

These were small fours of L-head monobloc configuration, modern for the period and an anticipation of what would be standard practice by 1914. Lubrication was of semi-pressure type, cooling was by thermo-siphon, and the Stoewers preferred wet-plate clutches.

Detail specifications varied: there were three speeds on the smallest B1 and four speeds on larger versions, which also used exhaust pressure fuel feed instead of gravity. B1s, though not B6s, had three-quarter-elliptic rear springs designed for the poor road conditions in Eastern Europe.

A wide range was offered in 1911, from a diminutive 1½-litre up to an enormous 8.8-litre six and a four-cylinder car with a Knight sleeve-valve engine purchased complete from Daimler of Coventry. The B6 was credited with 30 mpg (9.5 lit/100). Oil consumption, however, was in the region of 500 mpg (56 lit/100).

Delaunay-Belleville SMT
1912, France

With their round radiators as a reminder of their makers' origins – Delaunay-Belleville's marine boilers were world-famous – these cars were among the aristocrats of Edwardian motordom. One never drove a Delaunay – one was driven in it. Among those who favoured the breed were Indian princes, British peers, the President of the French Republic, the King of Greece and, above all, the last Tsar of All the Russias, whose garages contained 20 examples. His three flagships, delivered between 1909 and 1912, were the enormous SMTs. The designation stood for *Sa Majesté Le Tsar*, and the model was exclusive to him. No other crowned head could have one.

Even by Delaunay-Belleville's standards the cars were enormous – and their regular sixes were big enough. Top of the 1911 range was the 9.3-litre CA, and even in the 1914–20 period, when the age of monsters was over, there was still an 8-litre, the O-type, complete with twin transmission brakes, one at each end of the gearbox, and linked to twin pedals. The forward one was uncomfortably close to the flywheel, and caught fire easily. And while standard Delaunays no longer used chain drive, it was still found on the SMT. Wheelbase was 161 inches (4.08m), and the interior equipment included canteens, ashtrays and even matchboxes in solid silver, electric light and heaters. With that seven-bearing crankshaft of formidable length, one may hope that the car was never driven at high speeds.

If staid by reputation, the make was not devoid of advanced thinking. Even on the first four-cylinder cars, announced in 1904, full-pressure lubrication was used. Delaunays always featured comprehensive undershielding, and a Barbey compressed-air starter was a regular option. This could be employed to jack up the wheels, inflate the tyres, and blow a whistle. Monobloc engines were found on smaller Delaunays, magneto ignition was standard, and most models had four forward speeds. Electric lighting and demountable rims had made their appearance by 1913, and starters were available a year later. Medium-sized cars were not impossibly expensive: a 4.4-litre HB6 chassis cost £600 ($3,000) in England. Between 1908 and 1915 the firm turned out 3,754 of their sixes alone, an impressive record.

"The Car Magnificent"

Delaunay Belleville

The elegant, dignified, silent Delaunay Belleville—whether at Town Functions or on Country Tours—is the hall-mark of its owner's social position.

Delaunay Belleville Automobiles (England), Ltd., 49, Pall Mall, S.W.

'One doesn't drive a Delaunay-Belleville – it simply isn't done.' So they said in France, and this advertisement stresses the need for a chauffeur.

Rover 12hp
1912, Great Britain

In the years just prior to World War I the family car was taking shape. In Europe, there had of course been no such thing in the pioneer years, but with more dependable engineering came a flood of middle-class buyers. The British norm of 1912–15 can best be summarized as a '15.9hp' according to the RAC taxation formula. This meant a capacity of between 2.3 and 2.8 litres, four cylinders, side valves, cone clutch, three- or four-speed gearbox, and bevel drive. Such a vehicle would cruise comfortably at 35 mph (56km/h) and cost somewhere between £350 ($1,750) and £450 ($2,250). For this sum the client would expect hood, screen and detachable wheels, though he would also expect to pay extra for electric lighting. Starters were an unthinkable luxury before 1914.

Owen Clegg's Rover 12, new for 1912, came close to such parameters. True, cylinders of 75mm bore made it a 14 for tax purposes, but this had little significance as long as taxation was low. Clegg considered three forward speeds sufficient; like Lanchester, he also preferred the quiet and durable worm-drive axle. A transmission brake was retained, and the cylinder head was non-detachable, but in other respects the side-valve monobloc engine was very modern, with integral manifolding, a carburetter bolted direct to the

block, and even an oil dipstick, a real novelty for these days. Wheelbase was 110 inches (2.8m), sufficient for roomy five-seater bodies, the steel wheels were detachable and electric lighting was part of his £350 ($1,850) package. With a top speed of 43 mph (69km/h) the car would cruise at the desired velocity, while at 2,408lb (just under 1,100kg) it was not excessively heavy.

It also put the famous Coventry firm well and truly on the map. Rover had done fairly well in early days with their simple single-cylinder runabouts, and their 20hp four had won the 1907 Tourist Trophy, but the singles had gone on too long, and a line of small sleeve-valve machinery had not helped. Clegg noted that the fours were the best-sellers, and scrapped the existing five-model range in favour of two such types, the 12 and a 3.3-litre 18.

By mid-1912, however, he had been seduced across the Channel by Darracq, also in trouble through involvement with 'valveless' engines, albeit of a different type. He rescued them with what amounted to a carbon copy of the Rover, but his work in England had been well done, and that company's 12 sold 1,943 units in 1914. In improved form with full electrics, it would be revived after the war, as a 14, and produced until 1924.

► *The front end of the Rover.*
Full integration of body and
chassis is still a long way
away, and there is no smooth
line from firewall to bonnet.
The mascot in this case is not
Rover's traditional Viking.
The electric lighting is worth
noting: by 1915 the
headlamps would be rigidly
attached to the radiator—
advanced practice for those
days.

▼ *The large-diameter wheels,*
comprehensive weather
protection and high ground
clearance identify this Rover
as a 'Colonial' model, a
regular addition to European
makers' ranges in pre-1914
days. Not visible are the
stiffer springs. Unusually, this
car has acetylene lighting,
with the generator on the
running board.

Russo-Baltique Model-K
1912, Russia

Argyll 25/50hp
1913, Great Britain

Most of Tsarist Russia's wealthy motorists bought French or German, though they also liked the English Vauxhall. Yet the Russo-Baltic Wagon Works of Riga (whose principal business was railway rolling stock) turned out over 500 cars and maybe 250 trucks between 1906 and 1915. What is more, the vehicles, though designed by Swiss and German engineers, were built almost in their entirety in Russia. Carburetters and magnetos were imported; so, initially, were radiators and tyres, but by 1911 the Prowodnik rubber company not only supplied Russo-Baltic: they were exporting tyres to the West.

Julien Potterat, from Fondu of Belgium, was the first chief engineer, producing a conventional $4\frac{1}{2}$-litre four with side valves in a T-head, three-speed gearbox, semi-elliptic springs, and shaft drive. The car was known as the Russo-Baltique. Among the customers was the Tsar, while André Nagel, a Russian motoring journalist, entered a Russo-Baltique for the 1912 Monte Carlo Rally and finished in ninth place.

Potterat was succeeded by Ernst Valentin from the German Rex-Simplex factory, who improved the 24 with more power and an extra forward gear. He also added the big 7.4-litre Model-K to the range. Negotiations were opened for the licence-production of Spanish Hispano-Suizas, but World War I supervened. A handful of modified 24/40 Russo-Baltiques was built at Fili in 1922 under the Prom-Bron name, using tools and equipment removed from Riga before the Revolution of 1917.

Argyll were one of the unluckiest – and the worst managed – firms in history. The Scottish makers were good for 1,000 cars a year by 1905. But then they moved into the enormous and uneconomic Alexandria Works, the chief engineer, Alex Govan, died young, and ultimately the whole empire crashed in the summer of 1914, after losses estimated at £15,000 ($75,000) a quarter.

The 1913 cars deserved better. These used the Burt single-sleeve-valve engine, in which the sleeve underwent a twisting motion giving the minimum of wear. As quiet as the Knight used by Daimler and Minerva, it smoked less and consumed less oil. But it was just as expensive to build – and Argyll had to defend it in court against the Knight patentees.

Further, Argylls came with Rubury four-wheel brakes as standard. These, unlike the rival systems of Crossley and Isotta Fraschini, were coupled, both pedal and lever working on all wheels. For the rest, the 25/50's 4.1-litre engine developed 50bhp at 2,000rpm, had dual ignition, and delivered its power via a four-speed separate gearbox and torque tube to an overhead worm back axle. The Argyll-built bodies were streamlined for the day, detachable wire wheels and electric lighting were regular equipment, and the range included two wheelbase lengths: 126 inches (3.2 m) for tourers, and 135 inches (3.42 m) for formal carriages. There was also a Colonial model with bigger ground clearance.

1913 Argyll 25/50 hp

Gräf und Stift 40/45
1913, Austria

The 'Rolls-Royce of Austria' wore a silver lion on its radiator cap. It would still be wearing one in the mid-30s, when the firm's luxury straight-eights were supplemented by a cheap line of licence-built Citroëns, on which it looked incongruous. But in Habsburg days it was the chosen carriage of the Emperor Franz Josef II, while his successor, the ill-fated Karl, took the 40/45 illustrated below into exile with him.

As early as 1897 the brothers Gräf had built a small front-wheel drive runabout, before manufacturing a series of cars for Arnold Spitz, a Viennese importer. The Gräf und Stift name was not used until Spitz went bankrupt in 1907.

Their products were big and luxurious, and made in modest numbers. Common to the whole range were pair-cast four-cylinder engines with side valves in a T-head, pump and fan cooling, magneto ignition, splash lubrication, and exhaust pressure fuel feed. The transmission line included a leather cone clutch and separate four-speed gearbox, while the bigger types had twin transmission brakes. This arrangement resulted in five pedals, the others being clutch, accelerator, and exhaust cutout. Most interesting of all, though peculiar to the 40/50 hp, was the use of a de Dion rear axle (see page 24). On 50 bhp, the Gräf und Stift was good for over 60 mph (105 km/h).

1913 Gräf und Stift 40/45

Gräf und Stift's silver lion mascot.

Hillman 9.5 hp
1913, Great Britain

By 1913, the big car in miniature was becoming popular: even America had one, in the shape of the Saxon (opposite). Typical of the British idiom, if perhaps less common than Morris, Singer or Standard, was A. J. Dawson's 9.5 hp Hillman, of which 450 were sold in 1914.

The 1.4-litre L-head monobloc engine had a two-bearing crankshaft, magneto ignition, and gravity feed from a tank on the streamlined dash. The usual cone clutch and three-speed gearbox transmitted the power to an overhead worm back axle, springs were semi-elliptic and wheels of steel detachable type. For £200 ($1,000) one got a hood, windscreen, number plates, tools and spare wheel complete with tyre; only the side and tail lamps (and, curiously, the horn) were electrified. The Hillman would put 25 miles (40 km) into the hour under normal road conditions, and return 30–35 mpg (8–9.4 lit/100).

Competition was fierce: in 1914 the Hillman had eight direct native rivals, from AC to Standard, plus two from France (Clément-Bayard and de Dion-Bouton) and the Mathis from Germany. Cheapest of the lot was the Humberette, but its vee-twin engine put it in the cyclecar class despite its conventional driveline. Hillman could not compete against Calthorpe and Morris, with respective prices of £168 ($840) and £175 ($875). Thus for 1915 the company moved up a class with a 102-inch (2.59 m) wheelbase, 1.6-litre engine, and full electrics, including a starter. This 11 hp would form the basis for post-war production.

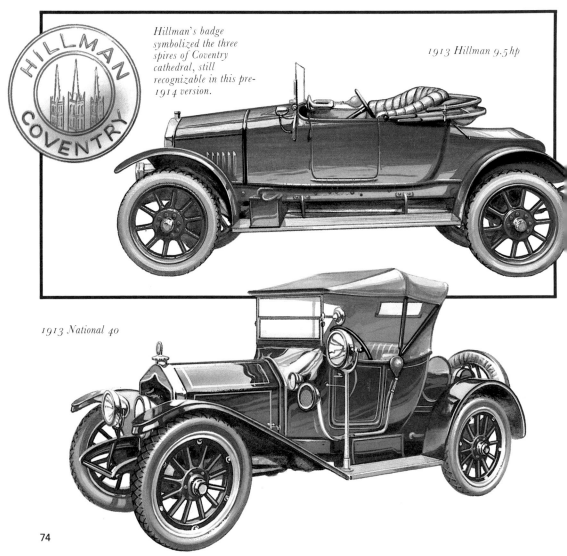

Hillman's badge symbolized the three spires of Coventry cathedral, still recognizable in this pre-1914 version.

1913 Hillman 9.5 hp

1913 National 40

National 40
1913, United States

Just before World War I America was making splendid, if spartan sports cars like Mercer, Stutz, and the huge chain-drive Simplex. This was a logical aspect of standardization. With stereotyped automobiles being turned out in vast quantities, there were customers who wanted something different, and were prepared to pay over $2,000 (£400) for it.

Highly respected was the National from Indianapolis, product of a firm which had tried air cooling and battery-electric cars in its time; it would fade out with an abortive light plane in the mid-30s. National's 1913 offering was a curious mixture of ancient and modern.

Under the bonnet was a hefty pair-cast four of the old T-head configuration, with air-pressure feed from a big rear tank, and dual ignition with two sets of spark plugs. Wheels were fixed, with demountable rims, but there was no transmission brake. Three forward speeds sufficed: controls were standard American, with left-hand steering and central change. Electric lights and an electric starter were inclusive at the list price of $3,150 (£630), while an interesting refinement was the engine-driven tyre pump, a boon when inflating those big 36-inch tyres!

National's 1913 catalogue claimed 187 firsts, 114 seconds and 79 third places in recent competitions. 'Race victories', they said, 'do not stop at the end of the race. They live forever in the character of the car and the way it is built'.

Saxon Four
1913, United States

America had a brief cyclecar craze, though the conventional small car was rare in a land of low taxes and cheap fuel. The successful Saxon was, however, European in capacity and dimensions. Its 1½-litre four-cylinder Continental engine was essentially the same as that fitted to 1915–19 Morris-Cowleys; wheelbase was a modest 96 inches (2.438m); weight was only 1,150lb (525kg); and it was offered only as a two-seater. The factory's claims included 35mpg (8lit/100) and 200 miles to the *quart* of oil, a sad commentary on the unfrugal habits of splash systems! Tyre consumption was said to be low.

The simple side-valve engine was cooled by thermo-siphon. Coil ignition was preferred to a magneto, and for the $395 (£79) asked in 1913 the customer got neither electrics nor instruments. Windscreen and tool kit were, however, included, and the cycle-type wire wheels soon gave way to the usual wood artilleries. To save money, Saxons made do with a two-speed transaxle, gear change was of the outmoded quadrant type, and springs were quarter-elliptic. With an eye on export markets, right-hand drive was available, and quite a few Saxons reached Britain, especially during the wartime American car boom of 1915–16. Over 30,000 of the original fours were turned out before the company switched, perhaps unwisely, to a small six in 1917.

Despite the adoption of assembly-line production, modest prices and a switch back to fours in 1920, the company folded in 1922.

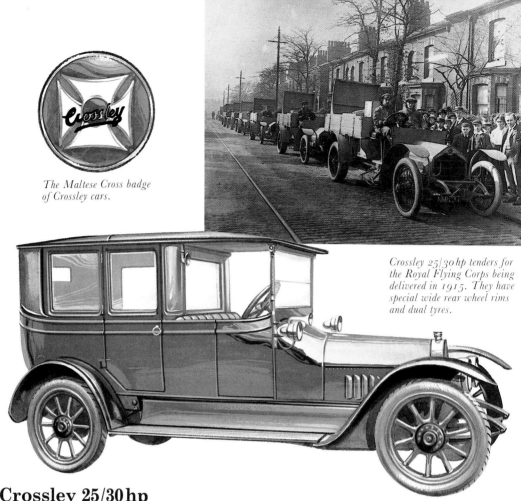

The Maltese Cross badge of Crossley cars.

Crossley 25/30 hp tenders for the Royal Flying Corps being delivered in 1915. They have special wide rear wheel rims and dual tyres.

Crossley 25/30 hp
1914, Great Britain

To British servicemen in World War I, the 25/30 Crossley was the equivalent of the Humber Super Snipe of 1939/45–a military maid of all work. It served as a staff car, ambulance, and, first and foremost, as the Royal Flying Corps's standard tender. Even after this Service became the Royal Air Force in 1918, the 'RFC' label clung to the car.

The Crossley was an odd case of technical regression. When first introduced for 1910, it had uncoupled four-wheel brakes, but these (unlike Argyll's more effective system) proved skid-prone and were dropped after a couple of seasons, leaving the 25/30 (and subsequent large four-cylinder Crossleys) to sit it out to the end on the old combination of a transmission footbrake and rear-wheel handbrake. The rest represented solid British engineering. The cylinders of the side-valve four-cylinder engine were cast in pairs, with semi-pressure lubrication, and a massive five-bearing crankshaft. Cooling was by thermo-siphon with fan

assistance, the high-tension magneto was backed by a coil, and the ratios of the four-speed gearbox were selected by a right-hand lever. Tubular cross members were used in the frame, and wheels were detachable: special wide rims and twin rear tyres identified military models. The Crossley was good for 60 mph (100 km/h) and 17 mpg (16.5 lit/100); sports models, distinguished by their 'trout-nose' (rounded-vee) radiators, were appreciably faster, and did well in pre-war sprints. This vee radiator was standardized on all 25/30s from 1919 onward.

Having been in continuous production throughout the war, Crossley were among the first British makers to resume deliveries after the Armistice. The 25/30 became the correct form of prestige transport in the Empire: several were used on the Prince of Wales's tour of India in 1921, and he subsequently owned two cars of this type. Four went to the King of Siam in 1922, while a pair of tenders was used by Major Court-Treatt on his Cape-London voyage in 1924–5.

Delage Type-AK
1914, France

The small six is generally regarded as a phenomenon of the late twenties and early thirties; in any case, the type generally had fallen out of favour around 1910. But a demand for ultra-flexible cars compact enough for a woman to drive had led to models of less than 3 litres capacity, available in 1914 from Loreley in Germany, Hillman in England, and

Front view of the Delage Type-AK.

LB9502

Delage in France. Louis Delage had started in 1905 with proprietary-engined singles, bludgeoning his way to fame by supporting races on a shoestring. He had been rewarded by victory in the 1907 *Coupe des Voiturettes* and between 1909 and 1914 he marketed some excellent 1½-litre fours.

Outwardly this new AK type resembled an elongated four, with its neatly streamlined dash incorporating external petrol and oil filler caps. The engine, too, was a neat, side-valve monobloc affair with integrally-cast manifolds, magneto ignition, and full-pressure feed for the three-bearing (formerly four-bearing) crankshaft. The clutch was a cone, and a four-speed gearbox soon replaced the three-speed type. Already Delage had relegated his transmission brake to a back-up role: the pedal worked in drums on the rear wheels. The maximum output of 30 bhp was delivered at 2,000 rpm, sufficient to give a top-gear range of 6–50 mph (10–80 km/h); 40 mph (60–65 km/h) was, however, a comfortable cruising gait, and a gallon of petrol lasted 22 miles (13 lit/100).

Though primarily aimed at the owner driver, it was available in wheelbases up to 132 inches (3.38 m) for formal bodies, electric lighting was standard, and starters a regular option. Total production is not known, but was probably in the region of 500–600 units in four seasons.

1914 Delage Type-AK

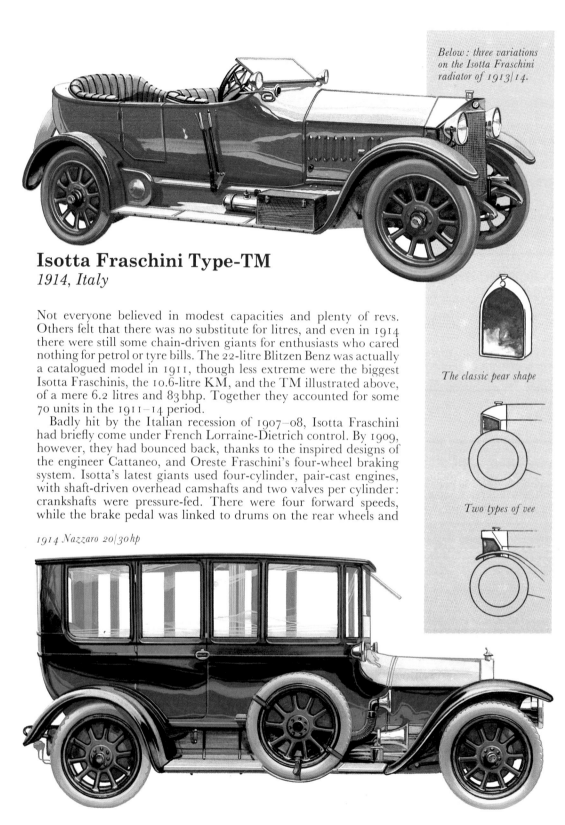

Below: three variations
on the Isotta Fraschini
radiator of 1913/14.

Isotta Fraschini Type-TM
1914, Italy

The classic pear shape

Two types of vee

Not everyone believed in modest capacities and plenty of revs. Others felt that there was no substitute for litres, and even in 1914 there were still some chain-driven giants for enthusiasts who cared nothing for petrol or tyre bills. The 22-litre Blitzen Benz was actually a catalogued model in 1911, though less extreme were the biggest Isotta Fraschinis, the 10.6-litre KM, and the TM illustrated above, of a mere 6.2 litres and 83 bhp. Together they accounted for some 70 units in the 1911–14 period.

Badly hit by the Italian recession of 1907–08, Isotta Fraschini had briefly come under French Lorraine-Dietrich control. By 1909, however, they had bounced back, thanks to the inspired designs of the engineer Cattaneo, and Oreste Fraschini's four-wheel braking system. Isotta's latest giants used four-cylinder, pair-cast engines, with shaft-driven overhead camshafts and two valves per cylinder: crankshafts were pressure-fed. There were four forward speeds, while the brake pedal was linked to drums on the rear wheels and

1914 Nazzaro 20/30 hp

transmission: the lever worked on the front wheels only.

For a chassis price of £1,400 in England or $9,000 in the United States, the KM offered 140 bhp and nearly 100 mph (160 km/h), together with a surprising docility. The customer had a choice of three different radiator styles: a pear shape very like that of contemporary Fiats, an aggressive German-style vee, and a gentler vee curiously anticipatory of the post-War 3-litre Bentley. The smaller TM was credited with 70 mph (112 km/h). Just before World War I a shaft-drive edition (Type TC) was offered. After the war, Isotta Fraschini's product, one of the world's first straight eights, became luxurious rather than sporty in character.

Nazzaro 20/30 hp
1914, Italy

Italy's speciality was still the luxury touring car, the medium bracket being typified by the 4½-litre '20/30s' offered by nine firms in 1913/14. Common to all were four cylinders, side valves (usually in an L-head, and cast monobloc), magneto ignition, four-speed gearboxes with right-hand change, and bevel drive. Advertised outputs were in the 30–40 bhp sector, delivered at around 1,500 rpm, and a 3-metre (118-inch) wheelbase was the norm. Further, many of them were look-alikes, with Mercedes-style radiators being phased out in favour of the new pear shape.

Among those who took on the established names (Bianchi, Fiat, Isotta Fraschini, SPA and Züst) was racing driver Felice Nazzaro, long the star of the Fiat works team. His designer was the Swiss, Arnold Zoller, later a pioneer of supercharging, and the Nazzaro was an excellent, if conventional, automobile. Its three-bearing crankshaft was pressure-lubricated, cooling was by pump, and there was a liberal aluminium content (crankcase, gearbox casing, dash, footboards). The clutch was a multiple dry plate, Nazzaro preferred three-quarter-elliptic springs at the rear, and (remarkably) both sets of brakes worked in finned drums on the rear wheels. Detachable steel wheels were standard. Electric lighting was an optional extra in 1914, and the short-chassis Nazzaro Corsa with two-seater body was said to be good for 75 mph (120 km/h).

Alas, Nazzaro was less successful as a manufacturer than as a driver, and he had had enough of building cars by 1916. In any case, the war had halted production after only 230 20/30s had been delivered.

Ohio Electric
1914, United States

Last stronghold of the battery-electric passenger car was the United States, partly because with such a huge motoring population (1,623,739 cars registered in 1914), even a tiny, conservative minority spelt a sizeable overall demand. In the 1909–15 period, the number of electric-car makers never fell below 20, reaching its zenith in 1912, with 27 such firms in the field.

The formula was stereotyped. A series-wound electric motor was mounted under the floor amidships, driving to a differential axle. Body shape was dictated to a large extent by

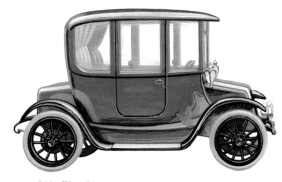

1914 Ohio Electric

the exigencies of battery stowage, hence the front and rear 'boots'. The base motive power also applied to brakes, gear shift, and even, on some Ohios, to the windows. Also advanced was the curved windscreen, though safety glass was as yet unknown. Maximum performance could be pursued either forwards or backwards, and the electric's lever control enabled it to be conducted from front or rear seat. Though cushion tyres were still listed in 1914, pneumatics were general practice.

Prices were high. At a time when $1,050 (£210) would buy a Buick touring car and $1,575 (£315) a Studebaker Six, both with full electrics, the average electric brougham cost around $3,000 (£600), or more than a closed Cadillac. Open runabouts cost less – Detroit, the leading makers, had one at $2,300 (£460) – but these were seldom encountered. Fuel rationing never hit the United States in World War I, and by the end of the 1920s, only Detroit of the electric car makers were still in business, making the odd vehicle to special order, usually with petrol-car styled bonnet.

Peugeot Bébé
1914, France

Smallest of the new 'big cars in miniature' was Peugeot's Bébé, launched in 1912, and designed by none less than Ettore Bugatti. In production form it made do with two speeds, instead of the five envisaged by its creator.

This was a real miniature on a wheelbase of 71 inches (1.8 m), and 103 inches (2.62 m) long. The engine, an 856 cc T-head four, gave 10 bhp and would run up to 2,000 rpm. Bugatti-type reversed quarter-elliptic rear suspension was to be expected, but the transmission was ingenious, consisting of two concentric propeller shafts driving bevels, the selection of the ratios being effected by a sliding dog-clutch at the forward end of the propeller shaft. A separate lever was furnished for reverse. A small gearbox was later added in front of the torque tube to transform the vehicle into a three-speeder: it coped with first and reverse. The drip-feed lubricators were tucked away under a streamlined dash and one took one's eye off the road to consult them.

With a top speed of only 35 mph (56 km/h), a lack of directional stability mattered little. Better news was a tyre consumption estimated at 6,000 miles (nearly 10,000 km) a set. The model was in production until 1916, by which time 3,095 had been made. After the war the Bébé was replaced by a more conventional car with L-head engine, differential-less back axle, and a track so narrow that seats had either to be staggered or set in tandem.

Protos 27/65 PS
1914, Germany

Germans, like Italians, were addicted to large cars, the difference being that the former nation sold them at home. Hence no fewer than sixteen models were available in 1914 with capacities in excess of seven litres and advertised outputs between 60 and 105 bhp. In this class speeds of 70 mph (112 km/h) were commonplace, while mechanical specifications embraced everything from T-head hangovers up to the single overhead camshaft of Mercedes's latest 28/95. At 7.2 litres, this last was not much bigger than the heaviest Protos.

That company had been building shaft-drive sixes since 1905. It had raced the type, albeit without success, in the 1907 Kaiserpreis. While the company's entry for the New York-Paris race was a four, sixes went to the House of Hohenzollern: both the Kaiser and the Crown Prince were customers. Protos's designer was the same Ernst Valentin who subsequently worked for Russo-Baltique (see page 72).

Valentin's engines were of T-head type, cast in pairs, and things changed little after his departure. The pump cooling, dual ignition, and exhaust pressure feed typified this class of car, rear springs were three-quarter-elliptic and the wood wheels wore demountable rims. A heavy vehicle – the chassis alone weighed over 3,000 lb (1,400 kg) – the Protos was not a spectacular performer. By 1914, familiar improvements were creeping in, notably a more modern L-head power unit. Also present were electric lighting and starting, friction-type shock absorbers, and a power tyre pump. In 14 pre-war years, Protos made approximately 10,000 cars.

1914 Peugeot Bébé

An early Peugeot lion mascot. On later cars (from 1920) the lion stood upright.

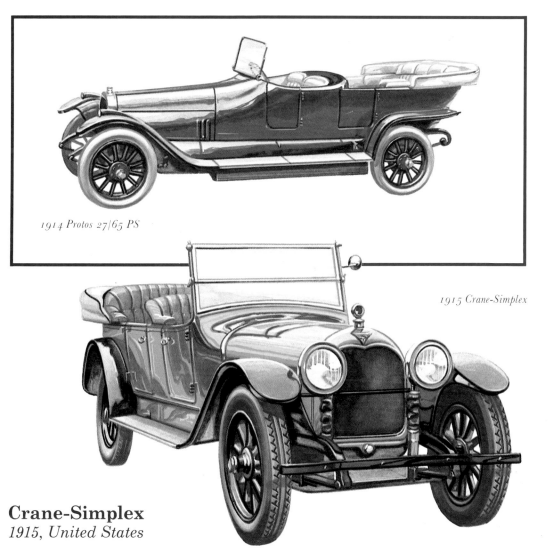

1914 Protos 27/65 PS

1915 Crane-Simplex

Crane-Simplex
1915, United States

Up to 1911, America imported many of her luxury cars, but the rise of the native strain, notably the 'three P's' (Packard, Peerless and Pierce-Arrow), was apparent by 1915, when the state of Massachusetts registered 3,102 Packards and 794 Pierces, but less than 200 Fiats, the most popular foreign breed.

In 1915, Simplex were ready to scrap their chain-drive sports cars. Their successor, designed by Henry M. Crane, cost $6,500 (£1,300) complete. It had six cylinders where the old Simplexes had been content with four, and came on a wheelbase of 143½ inches (3.64 m). It was also guaranteed for life while in the original owner's possession; this confidence seems to have been warranted, for trouble-free mileages of 350,000 miles (560,000 km) have been recorded.

Even with pressure lubrication, three main bearings sound inadequate on a vast 9-litre engine, but this was conservatively rated, delivering its 110 bhp at 2,000 rpm. Exhaust pressure feed and pump cooling were fairly general practice, but European influences were apparent in the 12-volt electrics, four-speed gearbox, and transmission footbrake. The spiral bevel back axle was a sign of the times, and of course the car had left-hand steering with central control. With its 'stream line dash' the Crane-Simplex could pass as a 1921 model, and indeed survived uneasily without change into 1924. For a while it formed part of E. S. Hare's luxury-car empire, along with Locomobile and Mercer. One could not, however, emulate General Motors without a Chevrolet in one's locker . . . .

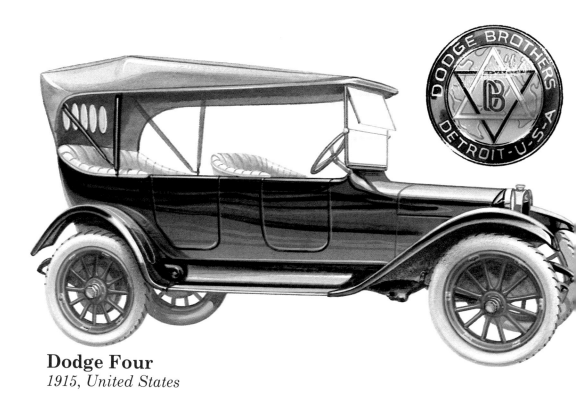

Dodge Four
1915, United States

To launch a new make of cheap automobile two months after the outbreak of a world war, as Dodge did, seems foolhardy. But when that make comes third in the national sales stakes in its first full season, and doubles these sales within two years, it becomes hard to credit.

In the United States, however, military involvement seemed very far away in 1914. Even when President Woodrow Wilson brought the country into the conflict on the Allied side in 1917, civilian production was merely curtailed. And in the intervening years, a technical head start had been matched by formidable export sales. America had cashed in on the car shortage: Britain was taking 4,000 vehicles a month at peak in 1915. There were also places like the Antipodes and South America where Detroit's wares were tailor-made for local conditions, and base price was low enough not to be inflated to ridiculous levels by import duty and freight. Dodges, too, appealed to the Army. The 250 supplied for General Pershing's Mexican expedition in 1916 proved so tough that at least another 9,000 were supplied in the ensuing two years.

The civilian customer, who paid $785 (£157) for his touring or roadster in 1915, got something better than a Ford. Common to both species was a big, slow-turning L-head monobloc four, with detachable head, though Dodge's was bigger (3.5 as against 2.9 litres), and more powerful at 35 bhp. But where Ford stayed with two speeds, Dodge favoured a conventional driveline with a cone clutch and three-speed gearbox. The rear-wheel brakes worked better than Ford's, a starter was standard, and though Dodge's longitudinal suspension was perhaps less tolerant of really impossible going, it could still cope with the rough stuff and give a reasonable highway ride. A sweeter, multiplate clutch was soon adopted, though for many years the make had its own idiosyncrasies – 12-volt electrics instead of the now universal 6-volt, and a back-to-front gear change, with the two higher ratios on the 'wrong' side. (Buick in America and Wolseley in Britain were other long-standing subscribers to this heresy.)

The Dodge Four was destined for a 14-year run, just surviving Chrysler's 1928 takeover. Thereafter it lingered for a further few years in the truck range, and there was even an attempt to revive it as an export-only item in 1932, using Plymouth components. Production passed the 100,000-a-year mark for the first time in 1919, and peaked at 265,000 in 1926. Sedans appeared in 1916 (they were all-steel from 1919) and light commercials took their bow in 1917.

Even in 1915 it was possible to add extras (not always factory-approved) to one's Dodge. This example is certainly laden!

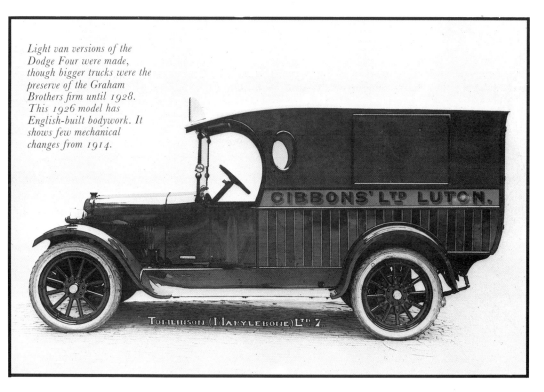

Light van versions of the Dodge Four were made, though bigger trucks were the preserve of the Graham Brothers firm until 1928. This 1926 model has English-built bodywork. It shows few mechanical changes from 1914.

Apperson 8-16
1916, United States

The compact vee-eight engine had been pioneered in France by de Dion-Bouton in 1910, and successfully commercialized five years later by Cadillac in America. By 1916 proprietary V8 engines were bringing the idiom within the reach of lesser firms, though Apperson, of Kokomo, Indiana, made their own, as befitted a pioneer name.

The brothers Edgar and Elmer Apperson were bush mechanics with a railroad background. They had been sponsored by a judge's son, Elwood Haynes, and their prentice experiments of 1894 had grown into a business making two cars a week by 1898. In 1902, however, the Appersons went their own way, progressing via horizontally-opposed, chain-drive twins to big conventional fours. By 1914 they had a six as well, though pro-

duction was always modest. 1916 would be their best year, with 2,000 of the new eights delivered.

B. J. Hubbard, Apperson's designer, set his two cylinder blocks at 90 degrees, with side valves (of course), fixed heads, and pressure lubrication. The rest of the specification was almost predictable—6-volt coil ignition, full electrics, a plate clutch, a three-speed gearbox with central change, a spiral bevel back axle, and rear-wheel brakes. Wheelbase was a generous 128 inches (3.25m), and if an 0–40mph (0–64km/h) acceleration time of 20 seconds sounds unimpressive by modern standards, this figure was achieved in top alone, a boon to those who could not double-declutch! At $1,850 (£370), the 8–16 was cheaper than a Cadillac.

Unfortunately, General Motors already offered cheaper V8s (Oakland, Oldsmobile), and Apperson could not compete. They closed their doors in 1926.

1916 Apperson 8-16

1916 Fiat Tipo 70

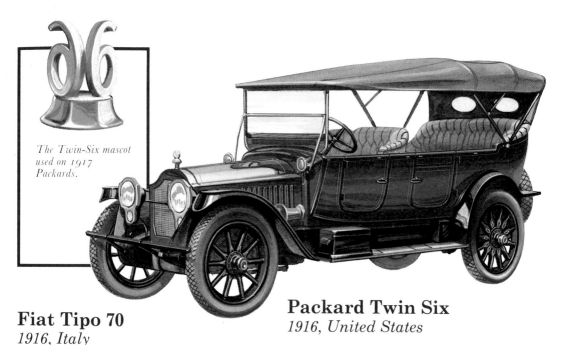

The Twin-Six mascot used on 1917 Packards.

Fiat Tipo 70
1916, Italy

Here is a true transitional model, bridging the gap between Veteran and Vintage. Though just over 1,000 Tipo 70s were built, and production continued into 1920, few ventured outside their native Italy.

In some respects the Tipo 70 is a car of the early 1920s. The dash is fully streamlined and properly instrumented. Most of the accepted 'Vintage' refinements are present: steel detachable wheels, and 12-volt lighting and starting. Although full-pressure lubrication has yet to come, the three-bearing side-valve engine has a detachable head, and the transmission brake has gone, replaced by two sets of shoes on the rear wheels. Of other familiar features, the magneto still has nearly a decade to go, and so has the simple gravity feed from a tank on the dash. Spiral bevel rear axles will be seen on the true post-war 501, and as yet two litres are seen as the minimum for a family car.

As originally laid down, the 70 had a two-bearing crankshaft and a non-detachable head. It even had the older, Mercedes style of radiator, already dropped from all but the smallest Fiats in 1915. The model's discontinuation immediately after the war was undoubtedly due to Giovanni Agnelli's foresight in recognizing the trend towards higher taxes, and his 1½-litre 501 did everything a 70 did: it cruised quietly at 35 mph (56 km/h). For those who wanted something bigger, there was the parallel 505 of 2.3 litres capacity, with room for seven on a 120-inch (3.048 m) wheelbase.

Packard Twin Six
1916, United States

Greater refinement and flexibility meant more cylinders. Thus the next step forward was a V12. Packard was first, followed by Weidely's proprietary, off-the-peg unit which spawned a flood of short-lived cars of no particular distinction.

The Twin Six, brainchild of J. G. Vincent, was intensively tested, a prototype averaging 15 mpg (18.8 lit/100) over 2,800 road miles. The engine's two blocks were set at an angle of 60 degrees, narrower than a regular (90-degree) V8; there was full-pressure lubrication; and the crankshaft incorporated a Lanchester vibration damper. The carburetter lived in the angle of the blocks, cooling was by twin water pumps, and output was 85 bhp from 7 litres. Packard's traditional transaxle was scrapped in favour of a three-speed unit box: the left-hand, remote-control change was, however, short-lived. All brakes were on the rear wheels, and final drive was by spiral bevel. A power tyre pump was provided as well as full electrics. The car would accelerate to 30 mph (50 km/h) in high gear in 12 seconds. Cylinder heads, fixed in 1916, were made detachable on 1919's Second Series.

A touring car was quite cheap at $3,150 (£630), although post-War inflation and import duty had pushed this up to £2,250 (the equivalent of over $11,000) by the time the model reached Britain in 1920. Over 35,000 Twin Sixes were sold before the model gave way to an even better straight 8 in 1923. In 1921, Warren G. Harding became the first American President to motor to his inauguration – in a 12-cylinder Packard.

Fageol
1917, United States

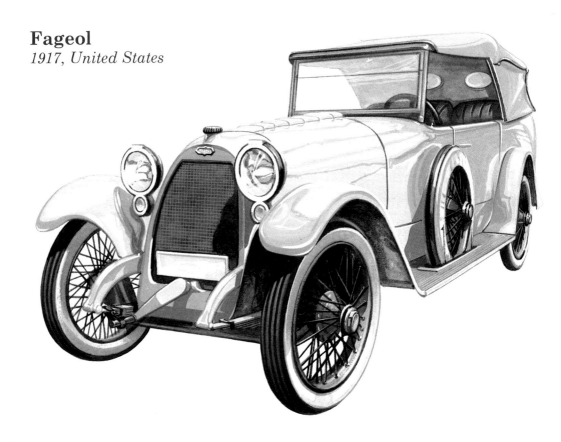

Traditionally aeronautical influences–overhead camshaft engines and the wider use of light alloys–belong to the Vintage period, while actual aero-engined cars are associated with record work. The high torque and effortless slow running of inline aero motors has, however, a fascination for those who like to travel fast and far, and the application remained viable until designers started to invert these power units in the cause of better streamlining. The snag, of course, was tax: a big-displacement motor such as the $13\frac{1}{2}$-litre Hall-Scott Six in the 1917 Fageol would have been rated at 60 hp in the United States or Britain.

The point was, unfortunately, academic. America's entry into World War I meant that the military wanted Hall-Scott motors in quantity, and the estimate of 20 Fageols built is almost certainly optimistic.

This was a pity, for the car was an engaging monster, and elegant with its wire wheels, sloping radiator, and dinosaur-like opening louvres on the bonnet top. The engine was of overhead-camshaft type with 12 valves, separate cylinders, and ignition by dual magnetos.

It developed its impressive 125 bhp at a low 1,300 rpm, and drove the bevel-drive back end via a three-speed gearbox; incredibly, a 1-to-1 axle ratio was a catalogued option. The chassis had side members six inches (15 cm) deep, some reinforcement being secured by mounting engine and gearbox on a bottle-shaped sub-frame. The brakes worked only on the rear wheels, though drums of 16-inch (407 mm) diameter gave a degree of confidence.

Refinement went more than skin-deep, as might be expected at a price of $13,500 (£2,700). Courtesy lamps illuminated the rear number plate, the engine, the running boards, the interior, and even the radiator badge. The badge, as well as the bonnet fasteners, was of carved ivory, while the tool box was lined in plush. Cruising speeds in the high 70s (120–125 km/h) were mentioned, though with high gearing and two-wheel brakes, the car was clearly intended to go rather than to stop.

F. R. Fageol later built trucks and advanced, high-speed motor coaches in Oakland, California.

Overland 4-90
1918, United States

Historically, a 1918 car qualifies as Veteran. Production examples from this year will, however, be American almost without exception. Anything European will be in the form of prototypes for the 1919 model run. In all its essential details, too, the 1918 Overland illustrated below right represents the sort of American automobile that would dominate world export markets over the next few years.

John North Willys had built up an obscure Indiana manufacture from bankruptcy to the Big League. Sales climbed from 4,860 in 1909 to a pre-war peak of 140,111 in 1916. Willys regularly took second place in sales behind Ford. He also built the middle-class Willys-Knight line, and was financially involved in

A 1920 version of the Overland Light Four with sedan body and detachable wire wheels.

many companies, including Curtiss Aircraft. In addition, he set up component firms like Tillotson (carburetters) and Autolite (electrics) to supply his plants. In 1920 he would make an unsuccessful attempt to manufacture cars in Britain, in association with Crossley of Manchester.

Overland cars had originally used two-speed planetary transmissions, but these had been dropped after 1912. The standard offering now featured a conventional three-speed gearbox, cone clutch, bevel drive, and rear-wheel brakes. From 1916 the separately cast cylinders of the traditional Overland engine had given way to a monobloc casting, while a year later magneto ignition had also gone, in favour of the universal 6-volt coil. Only in the suspension department was any heterodoxy apparent, for at front and rear the cars used pairs of splayed quarter-elliptics, closely akin to Ford's transverse set-up, and nearly as bouncy.

The Overland was rather more expensive than a Ford, and a touring car weighed 2,350 lb (1,067 kg) as against the Ford's 1,500 lb (665 kg). Further, post-war inflation raised the English price from the £225 ($1,125) asked in 1916 to a fearsome £475 ($2,375). The car did, however, have one advantage over Model-T. Though the latter was assembled in Britain, it was offered with left-hand drive only in the early post-war years, right up to the beginning of 1923, whereas Overlands could be had with right-hand steering.

TECHNICAL INFORMATION

Page	Make and Year	Capacity (cc)	No of Cylinders	Valves	Output (bhp)	No of Gears	Drive	Top Speed (mph/km/h)	Price in U.K. (Sterling)
14	1860 Rickett	na	2	slide	10	2	spur gear	18/29	not known
15	1885 Benz	985	1	slide	0·88	1	belt and chain	8/12	na
16	1885 Amédée Bollée	na	2	slide	not known	–	bevel	25/40	na
17	1893 Duryea	1,308	1	aiv	4	2	chain	10/16	na
18	1894 Panhard	1,060	2	aiv	4	3 or 4	chain	15/24	not known
20	1896 Léon Bollée	640	1	aiv	3	3	belt	30/50	£150
20	1897 Cannstatt Daimler	1,060	2	aiv	4	4	belt and spur gear	14/22	£340
21	1897 De Dietrich	3,060	2	aiv	9	4	belt and bevel	20/32	na
22	1898 Decauville	479	2	aiv	3	2	bevel	30/50	£185
22	1898 Pennington	1,196	1	aiv	3·5	1 or 2	rope and chain	not quoted	£99·75
23	1898 Saurer	3,140	1	aiv	6	3	chain	18/30	£550
24	1900 De Dion-Bouton	499	1	aiv	4·5	2	spur gear	30/50	£210
26	1900 Locomobile	na	2	slide	5-10	–	chain	25/40	£190
27	1900 Lohner-Porsche	na	na	na	10	3 or 4	hub motors	40/64	not known
28	1900 Serpollet	na	4	poppet	5	–	chain	35/56	£600
29	1901 Arrol-Johnston	3,042	2	aiv	12	4	chain	20/32	£470
29	1901 Delahaye	1,330	1	aiv	7	3	belt and chain	20/32	not known
30	1901 Mercedes	5,900	4	side, T-head	35	4	chain	50/80	na
32	1902 Scania	not known	1	aiv	not known	2 or 3	chain	not known	na
32	1902 Wolseley	2,601	2	aiv	10	4	chain	30/50	£380
34	1903 CGV	3,686	4	aiv	22	4	chain	40/65	not known
35	1903 Humberette	613	1	aiv	5	2	bevel	25/40	£131
36	1903 Lanchester	4,033	2	ohv	12	3	worm	38/61	£550
38	1903 Oldsmobile	1,563	1	ohv	5	2	chain	20/32	£168
39	1904 Daimler	5,703	4	side, L-head	36	4	chain	50/80	£1,150
40	1904 Darracq	3,054	4	side, L-head	20	3	bevel	46/73	£460
40	1904 Franklin	1,760	4	aiv	10	2	chain	40/64	na
41	1904 Kriéger	na	na	na	9	6	spur gear	18/30	not known
42	1905 Horch	2,725	4	overhead inlet (ioe)	22	4	bevel	44/70	£525 (chassis)
42	1905 Lacoste et Battmann	698	1	aiv	6	2	bevel	25/40	£131
43	1905 White	na	2	slide	15	2	bevel	40/64	£550
44	1906 Maxwell	1,642	2	side, L-head	8	2	bevel	35/56	£173·25
44	1907 Hispano-Suiza	7,340	4	side, T-head	45	4	bevel	62/100	£800 (chassis)
46	1907 Itala	7,430	4	side, T-head	45	4	bevel	55/90	£1,000 (chassis)
47	1907 Laurin-Klement	4,854	8	side, L-head	40	4	bevel	50/80	na
47	1907 Pullcar	1,810	4	side, T-head	16	3	chain	24/38	£475
48	1907 Rolls-Royce	7,046	6	side, L-head	48	4	bevel	65/104	£985 (chassis)
50	1907 Standard	3,312	6	side, L-head	25	3	bevel	40/64	£470

Page	Make and Year	Capacity (cc)	No of Cylinders	Valves	Output (bhp)	No of Gears	Drive	Top Speed (mph/km/h)	Price in U.K. (Sterling)
50	1907 Turcat-Méry	8,495	4	side, L-head	40	4	chain	not known	na
51	1908 OTAV	863	1	aiv	5·5	2	chain and belt	30/50	£99·75
52	1908 Renault	1,060	2	side, L-head	9	3	bevel	35/56	£200
52	1908 Thomas	6,408	4	side, T-head	50	4	chain	65/108	na
53	1908 Vauxhall	3,053	4	side, L-head	38	4	bevel	55/90	£465
54	1909 Ford	2,898	4	side, L-head	20	2	bevel	40/64	£225
56	1909 Martini	1,122	4	ohc	12	3	bevel	40/64	£290
57	1909 Metz	880	2	side, L-head	10	variable	chain	30/50	na
57	1909 Sears	1,754	2	aiv	14	2	chain	25/40	na
58	1909 Sheffield-Simplex	7,046	6	side, L-head	45	2	bevel	60/100	£795
59	1909 Stanley	na	2	slide	10-20	—	direct	50/80	£375
60	1910 Le Zèbre	599	1	side, L-head	7	2	bevel	30/50	£145
61	1910 Minerva	2,324	4	double-sleeve	30	4	bevel	45/72	£375 (chassis)
62	1910 Napier	6,160	6	side, L-head	45	3	bevel	60/100	£765 (chassis)
64	1910 Phänomobil	880	2	side, L-head	7	2	chain	40/64	£116
65	1910 Spyker	1,106	2	side, T-head	7	3	bevel	not known	na
66	1911 Bédélia	1,055	2	aiv	9	2	belt	50/80	£94
66	1911 EMF	3,695	4	side, L-head	30	3	bevel	50/80	£278
67	1911 Métallurgique	4,903	4	side, L-head	60	4	bevel	80/128	£665
68	1911 Stoewer	2,025	4	side, L-head	22	4	bevel	47/75	£325
69	1912 Delaunay-Belleville	11,846	6	side, L-head	70	4	chain	60/100	na
70	1912 Rover	2,297	4	side, L-head	22	3	worm	43/69	£350
72	1912 Russo-Baltique	7,440	4	side, T-head	50	4	bevel	not known	na
72	1913 Argyll	4,084	4	single-sleeve	50	4	worm	50/80	£825
73	1913 Gräf und Stift	7,320	4	side, T-head	50	4	De Dion	65/108	na
74	1913 Hillman	1,357	4	side, L-head	18	3	worm	45/72	£200
75	1913 National	7,325	4	side, T-head	50	3	bevel	70/112	na
75	1913 Saxon	1,484	4	side, L-head	15	2	bevel	40/64	£105
76	1914 Crossley	4,536	4	side, L-head	50	4	bevel	60/100	£575
77	1914 Delage	2,669	6	side, L-head	30	4	bevel	50/80	£424
78	1914 Isotta Fraschini	6,235	4	ohc	83	4	chain	70/112	£1,040 (chassis)
79	1914 Nazzaro	4,398	4	side, L-head	36	4	bevel	55/90	£495 (chassis)
79	1914 Ohio	na	na	na	na	5	bevel or worm	22/35	na
80	1914 Peugeot	856	4	side, T-head	10	3	bevel	35/56	£160
80	1914 Protos	6,840	6	side, L-head	65	4	bevel	72/115	na
81	1915 Crane-Simplex	9,220	6	side, L-head	110	4	spiral bevel	65/108	na
82	1915 Dodge	3,478	4	side, L-head	32	3	bevel	45/72	£275
84	1916 Apperson	5,100	8	side, L-head	60	3	spiral bevel	65/108	na
85	1916 Fiat	2,001	4	side, L-head	21	4	bevel	45/72	na
85	1916 Packard	6,950	12	side, L-head	88	3	spiral bevel	80/128	na
86	1917 Fageol	13,529	6	ohc	125	3	spiral bevel	90/145	na
87	1918 Overland	2,927	4	side, L-head	32	3	bevel	45/72	£475

Index

Note: page numbers printed in *italics* refer to illustrations

ACKNOWLEDGEMENTS

Picture Research: Eric Inglefield and Elizabeth Rudoff

Photographs: BBC Hulton Picture Library 18 *(below left)*, 20 *(above)*, 43 *(above right)*, 64 *(above)*; National Motor Museum, Beaulieu 11 *(above left and above right)*, 12, 14 *(above)*, 15 *(above right)*, 16 *(right)*, 17 *(left)*, 18 *(below right)*, 19 *(below)*, 21 *(centre and below left)*, 23 *(above right)*, 25, 26 *(above right)*, 27 *(above)*, 28 *(above right and below left)*, 30 *(below)*, 31, 33 *(above)*, 34 *(above)*, 37 *(above and below)*, 38 *(above)*, 48 *(below)*, 49 *(above and below)*, 51 *(below left)*, 53 *(below right)*, 54, 55 *(below)*, 76 *(below right)*, 58 *(above)*, 62, 63 *(above and below)*, 66 *(above)*, 67 *(centre)*, 68 *(above)*, 71 *(both)*, 76 *(above)*, 77 *(above)*, 83 *(both)*, 87 *(left)*; Cyril Posthumus 69 *(left)*; Peter Roberts 37 *(centre)*, 39 *(right)*, 53 *(above right)*; Tony Stone Associates 8, 35 *(below right)*, 52 *(above right)*, cover.